This
Tragic Gospel

This
Tragic Gospel

How John Corrupted
the Heart
of Christianity

Louis A. Ruprecht Jr.

JOSSEY-BASS
A Wiley Imprint
www.josseybass.com

Published by Jossey-Bass
A Wiley Imprint
989 Market Street, San Francisco, CA 94103-1741—www.josseybass.com

Jossey-Bass books and products are available through most bookstores. To contact Jossey-Bass directly, call our Customer Care Department within the United States at 800-956-7739, outside the United States at 317-572-3986, or fax 317-572-4002.

Jossey-Bass also publishes its books in a variety of electronic formats. Some content that appears in print may not be available in electronic books.

All quotations from the New Testament are the author's own translations from the Greek.

Library of Congress Cataloging-in-Publication Data
Ruprecht, Louis A., Jr.
    This tragic gospel : how John corrupted the heart of Christianity/Louis A. Ruprecht Jr.
    p.   cm.
    Includes bibliographical references and index.
    ISBN 978-0-7879-8778-7 (cloth)
       1. Bible. N.T. Gospels—Criticism, interpretation, etc.   I. Title.
  BS2555.52.R87   2008
  226'.06—dc22

                                         2008013107

Printed in the United States of America
FIRST EDITION
HB Printing   10 9 8 7 6 5 4 3 2 1

CONTENTS

This book is dedicated to the memory
of
DR. BARNEY LEE JONES
June 11, 1920–April 12, 2005

"Look, Teacher, what wonderful stones and what wonderful buildings!"
—MARK 13:1

ACKNOWLEDGMENTS

I have been interested in tragedy all my life, but the serious study of the possible relationship between Greek drama and the Christian gospels dates to my years of graduate study at Emory University. While there, I had the marvelous privilege of working with some of the most gifted Greek translators of our generation, among them William Arrowsmith and Herb Golder, as well as a wonderfully creative New Testament scholar, Vernon Robbins, who had already made the case for these subtle Greek and Christian weavings. My thesis adviser, Jon Gunnemann, allowed me to write a very wide-ranging dissertation on these themes, but perhaps his greatest influence on me was aesthetic. I recall with special fondness the many hours spent in his office, where a copy of Albrecht Dürer's 1526 painting *The Four Holy Men* boasted an incredible image of Mark's face. He is depicted as radically different from the rest, his face half hidden in shadow and the look on his face a mingle of rage and pain and pity that marks him as the only genuine tragedian of the four. That image was often on my mind as I devoted the next two years to the project, with the assistance of a Charlotte W. Newcombe Dissertation Fellowship, which enabled me to reside in Greece as I did so, living less than a mile from the Theater of Dionysus, where it all began.

I first published an article in the *Journal of Religion and Literature* about the various canonical performances of Gethsemane and John's rejection of them, and it was after reading this article that George Lawler of Continuum Press contacted me, wondering if there were perhaps a book in this idea. There was, of course, and with his assistance it became my first book, a long analysis of tragedy's strange career in modern philosophy and theology. It won an award from the Conference on Christianity and Literature as "book of the year," for which I was very grateful indeed. But I had not yet begun to work on the noncanonical gospels or on the more recent debates about early Christian formation, and I had only just started working on the excavation in Crete, so the ideas that eventually coalesced in this book had not been formed.

It required a new academic home to inspire that new journey. In 2005, I was honored to be asked to join a new faculty in a new department of Religious Studies at Georgia State University. My colleagues there—Jonathan Herman, John Iskander, Kathryn McClymond, Christopher White, and our chair, Timothy Renick—have done much to create the congenial intellectual home in which I have felt far freer to experiment with new thoughts and new ways of imagining religious history. Our deans, Lauren Adamson and Carol Winkler, have been steadfast friends, both to our department and to me personally. The best laboratory for most humanistic experiments is the undergraduate classroom, and I am very much in the debt of a marvelous group of our students who enrolled on two separate occasions in a new course of my own design, titled "Jesus Inside and Outside the Gospels." It was through their spirited engagement with the material I was attempting to read that my own ideas about this book were sharpened and clarified. Many of their questions have inspired the answers I try to develop here.

My agent, Giles Anderson, has been a supremely thoughtful mentor, adviser, and friend. It was during my initial preparations for this new course that a long and fairly informal phone conversation developed into this idea, then a formal proposal, and then, in very short order, into the project of which this book is the culmination. None of this would have happened without him.

Giles connected me first to Julianna Gustafson at Jossey-Bass, and while the birth of her first child necessitated her departure from the project and the press, her spirited and gracious involvement lives on in its pages. Sheryl Fullerton took up the reins of the project, and her sure touch—light when it needed to be and firm when there was danger on the road—has served brilliantly to bring it safely back to the barn. But they were the simply herculean attentions of Catherine Craddock that really made this book what it is now. Cat performed a simply astonishing labor of love, viewing my original drafts almost as if they were puzzles, pulling them apart piece by piece and then cobbling them together in ways I had not imagined. As Cat invited me to turn the kaleidoscope through which I gazed at my own words, wonderful new patterns, unglimpsed by me before, came into startling focus. This book simply would not be what it is without her kindness, her thoughtful intelligence, and her artist's eye.

Clearly, many friends have had a hand in the sifting of this material and the crafting of this book. To the names that demand prominence here, others should be added, especially those students and friends who have agreed to read drafts of the manuscript and have graced me with their questions, challenges, and insights. A special word of thanks is owed to Jeannie Alexander, Michael Lippman, and Lori Anne Ferrell, each of whom helped transform this book with their loving attention. It was Lori Anne who made the decisive suggestion that I refer to John's work as an "evangel," not a "gospel," and when she said this, the key finally turned in the lock.

These acknowledgments began with an image of my time as a graduate student. But the seeds for all of this, for the work I do and the career I have landed upon, were planted years earlier, when I was a wide-eyed and rather unsophisticated undergraduate at Duke University. It was there that Professor Barney Jones took a special interest in me, especially in my writing. He devoted himself to me and to my work with a generosity that I only now see for what it was, since I too have become a professor in the interim. He offered me his intellectual friendship and almost immediately his personal friendship as well.

Barney was to be my first professor of biblical studies at Duke University, where, in an age of resurgent fundamentalism, he patiently walked us through the scholarly methods of biblical study, with its emphasis on archaeology and history. His influence on my life was enormous, and hardly on mine alone; he was arguably the single most beloved teacher at Duke University, and when he retired in 1984, an era passed with him. It was because of him that I changed my course of study, and he is without a doubt the main reason that I am a professor of comparative religion today. Barney Jones departed this earth just three years ago, and while I still find it difficult to refer to him in the past tense, his historical presence is marked and ongoing. That idea was fundamental to his own understanding of the Christian faith.

One of the most remarkable aspects of Barney Jones's scholarly presence was its unapologetic *humanism*. I do not mean that in the customary sense of the term, which fundamentalists, among others, have turned into yet another term of Christian abuse. Barney Jones was no *"secular* humanist." Rather, he remained ever mindful of the fact that *traditions* are constituted by *people,* people who ask critical questions of them, people who try to embody their precepts, and people who must always, always work tirelessly to pass them on. Barney Jones was painfully aware of the fact that we are, all of us, links in a chain that connects the present to the past and that for any religious person who is scripturally inclined and scripturally serious, the past lays a very special burden on the present. History matters, as does archaeology and all the rest. Because of what Barney Jones invited me to see in the Bible, I moved to Israel for a summer excavation and then to Greece for several years more, working as an archaeologist and later as a teacher.

My entire scholarly career developed in tandem with our deepening friendship, and I mark his passing with a sadness for which I still have not found the words, despite three years of meditation and search. Barney's voice was a constant comfort, his humane wisdom was unmatched, and his kindness was legendary. But Barney, who served as a chaplain both in the Second World War and in Korea, knew tragedy intimately. His surpassing resources of compassion came from that deeply tragic well.

This book is dedicated to the man and to his memory.

Atlanta, Georgia   L.A.R.

July 2008

The last temptation is the greatest treason
To do the right thing for the wrong reason.

—T. S. ELIOT, *MURDER IN THE CATHEDRAL*

This
Tragic Gospel

Introduction

All three of the synoptic Gospels make great efforts to leave us with faith.
But the very means they employ cannot help but leave us with questions.

—GLENN MOST, *DOUBTING THOMAS* (2005)

E
arly one morning in the especially hot summer of 1990,
I was working in one of the main trenches at an archaeological excavation on the Greek island of Crete. The
site is called Phalasarna, one of the more impressive of the
Hellenistic pirate harbors that was destroyed by a Roman army
serving under Pompey and Metellus, one or two generations
before another Roman provincial governor sentenced Jesus
of Nazareth to death. Working alone, I suddenly came upon a
layer where the sediment was literally filled with broken pottery fragments. Quite suddenly, there seemed to be more
pottery than dirt where I was working.

It was very early, and it was already very hot, and so I fell
into the hypnotic rhythm all archaeologists know—peeling away
layers of dirt, removing pottery shards one by one, and plac-
ing them in a bag set aside specifically for this trench and for
this surprising new layer of finds. One especially large fragment, otherwise nondescript, caught my attention for some

reason, and I stopped what I was doing to look more closely at it. It was obviously part of a largish ceramic bowl, perhaps four feet in diameter, and seemed to belong to the middle of the body of the bowl. As the morning sun crested the mountains and illuminated our trench, I saw more clearly what had unwittingly attracted my attention to begin with: it was a *fingerprint,* perfectly preserved in the clay. No doubt it was the fingerprint of the potter who had thrown the bowl, then removed it from his or her wheel to place it in a kiln for firing. And thus a simple and otherwise commonplace piece of unpainted everyday ware became priceless and unique. Here was the unwitting signature of an altogether unique human being who had lived over twenty-five hundred years ago. We will never know the name or anything else about this mysterious potter. And yet for all of that, here I stood in the presence of *a singular human trace.*

That unforgettable experience provides the metaphor that I would like to apply to everything that follows in this book. Too often when we refer to a scripture as a "human book," this statement is heard as somehow demoting it, making it seem less inspired or less divine. That is not my intention at all. Rather, to refer to the Bible as a collection of human books is to remind ourselves that these books were written *by* human beings and written *for* human beings. These books describe a very human world, one filled with the names of dramatic historical personages, like Caesar, and others about whom we know no more than I know about my pirate-potter; and they are filled with names of important cities, like Rome and Athens, about which we know a great deal, as well as others we know only by name. The Bible is best viewed as a human book because the traces of the fingerprints of so many human beings are still there, still visible in the texts when we take the time to look for them. The joy of discovery can be as rich for a Christian reader as it is for an archaeologist; in any case, the mystery and the passion that create such joy are the same. It is all part of the magnificent adventure of history, of bringing the past to light.

Let me begin with this important point. A scripture is a kind of devotional writing, nothing more and nothing less. Christianity is a *scriptural* religion. And Christians today claim to have received a special revelation about God and God's relationship to the world through a body of sacred writings they call the Old and New Testaments. As far as the New Testament goes, these texts were written by particular people (like Mark and John), in a particular language (Greek), at a particular place and time (the eastern Mediterranean in the early period of the Roman Empire). This means that Christianity is also a *historical* religion, and its founding documents are *historical documents*, regardless of how they may be represented in Sunday schools or from Christian pulpits. These scriptures are not timeless documents dropped down from on high, deliberately severed from their place, their time, their original language, and their relationship to one another. Some of the Old Testament prophets may claim to be speaking in God's name, using phrases like "Thus says the Lord," but the New Testament gospels do not speak this way. They tell us that they offer a story about Jesus, a story "according to" Mark, "according to" John, and so on. So they present themselves as historical

3

documents, and they require historical sensitivities from their readers. They are also texts that talk back to one another and argue with one another, so they need to be excavated and studied with special care. Nowhere is this clearer than when we read the Christian gospels, documents written one or two generations after Jesus lived.

Jesus lived and died as a Jew in a Greek and Roman world. The name "Christian" did not exist yet. We're not even sure what that name meant. The New Testament informs us (in Acts of the Apostles 11:26) that a group of Jesus followers in the Syrian city of Antioch first called themselves by that name, but we don't know what we most want to know— namely, what the name meant *to them.* It is a Greek name, deriving from the Greek *christos,* which might simply have been a translation of the Hebrew word *messiah,* or "anointed one." Some of these early "Christians," then, might simply have intended to call themselves "messianic Jews," Jews who believed that God's messiah had indeed come and had created a new world of possibilities when he left. What is clear is that being Jewish was not a problem for these people, and neither was being Greek.

Three hundred years later, everything had changed. Christian bishops preached sermons proclaiming that Jewish synagogues were houses of Satan. "Greek" had become synonymous with "pagan," nothing more and nothing less, and their temples were systematically closed or destroyed. And along the way, the name "Christian" had presumably changed its meaning too. Now it was the name for *a new religion,* a religion that desperately needed to establish its essential difference from Jewishness and Greekness alike. John's account of Jesus's life and death had a lot to do with these changes, as we will see. What I want to suggest is that something else of equal importance and even greater moment changed in that same three-hundred-year time period: the conception of Christian compassion. The all-inclusive, Jews-and-Greeks-together brand of Christianity gave way to a much harsher movement increasingly defined by a line-drawing, border-defining, heresy-hunting religiosity that became even more violent when it attained imperial power in Rome.

How did this happen? That is what this book will try to explain. The story I am attempting to tell may be sketched fairly simply in outline. I will apply the flesh tones in subsequent chapters, much as an archaeologist re-creates whole pots from broken fragments, and much as historians reconstruct real human lives from the always sketchy historical evidence such humans leave behind. What is clear is that Jesus's unexpected execution in Jerusalem was a scandal from which it took his followers some time to recover. They did not write his story down right away. Instead, they commemorated some of the most dramatic things he had said and done in orally circulating traditions, which were finally written down one or two generations after his death—which is to say when all the eyewitnesses to these events were dying off. Mark did this first, and Matthew and Luke did something similar. John, however, took a very different approach. He wrote an entirely new description of Jesus's personality and a new version of his life, drawing on alternative traditions of what Jesus said and did. Moreover, John did all of this intending not so much to supplement what the other gospel writers had done as to replace them and to subvert their claims to authority. When the later Christian church essentially chose John's version of Jesus over Mark's more haunting account, it dealt a death blow to an earlier conception of Christian compassion. As I hope to show, this John-centered spirituality, with its radical new conception of who Jesus was, became the gospel of choice among Protestant Christians in Luther's day (and not only his). It continues to be alive and well in those forms of Protestant worship that call themselves "evangelical" or "fundamentalist" today.

From Mark to John to Heresy

This Tragic Gospel is a title that invites readers to think about two words, *tragedy* and *gospel,* and the subtle relation between them. "*This* tragic gospel" invites us to ask *which* is the tragic gospel? This may well seem an odd question to ask. All too often, Christians in North America refer to "the gospel" as if there were only one. Of course, in actuality, there are four gospels in the New Testament (as well as scores of other ones that were written in the first several Christian centuries, as we will see later on). *Synoptic* is a Greek word that means "seeing with," in the sense of "seeing the same way." It is used to describe the gospels of Mark, Matthew, and Luke, to remind us of how similar these three gospels seem and how very different from them John's version is. I hope to make very clear in this book that John does not see Jesus the same way at all.

6

So there is not one gospel; there are many. They were not written by God; they were written by inspired men, men whose names we know and whose personalities we can glimpse in the writings they have left behind. In Mark's and John's case, as I hope to show, we can clearly see a great deal about them— and tantalizing glimpses of a great conflict.

The scandal of Jesus's unexpected execution in Jerusalem created a crisis among his earliest followers. As I've already indicated, they maintained orally circulating traditions of memorable things that Jesus said and did, but it was unclear how to maintain a religious movement in his absence. One such follower, Mark himself, who was separated from Jesus by a single generation, had a novel idea about how to answer that question and to meet that need. He literally invented a new literary genre, the Christian gospel. And it was the invention of that genre that helped turn Christianity into a religion that was dependent on Jewish and Greek literary models but independent of Judaism and Hellenism.

The genius of this first gospel, the gospel according to Mark, lies in the way it tells the story of Jesus's life and death, depicting them both as a tragedy, a tragic history of misrepresentation and misunderstanding. Mark's novelty lay in his decision to model his telling of Jesus's story on a powerful classical genre: Greek tragedy, a genre that was designed to create an emotional response in its audience, one in which pity and fear and compassion are essential. John turned that all around by reimagining Jesus's story as an "antitragedy"— what I will call an *evangel*—a telling that denied all of Mark's pathos and in this way brought fear, not pity and not compassion, to the foreground as the most fundamental Christian emotion.

In contending that Mark took his inspiration from Greek tragedy, I do not mean to suggest that Mark thought Jesus "looked like" Oedipus or Heracles or Ajax. It was more a matter of *thinking tragically* about human suffering and human fragility and the compassion these human realities demand. The Greeks knew one thing that the Hebrew scriptures were ambivalent about and that the Qur'an seems explicitly to deny in places: that the gods can befriend a man and he may still come to a terrible end. Human beings are fragile, and suffering is our common lot. Greek tragedy does not offer cheap promises or false hopes, and it does not believe that everything works out in the end. Neither did the earliest followers of Jesus, who knew better; their messiah had been killed, after all.

It is very easy to miss the subtle genius of Mark's achievement. He brilliantly combined those orally circulating traditions about Jesus, cobbled them together into an explosive and dynamic story, and cloaked the whole ministry of Jesus in a profound atmosphere of mystery. Mark's Jesus is a powerful wonder-worker who doesn't want people to talk about his miracles. Mark's Jesus is a powerful speaker, a passionate arguer, and a prophet who doesn't want anyone even to suspect that he is the messiah. Mark's Jesus is also—and this is unknown even to his closest followers—a "son of God." The more this mysterious figure tries to keep a low profile, the more the crowds gather and gossip and speculate. Before anyone can understand quite what in the world has happened or who he is, Jesus is gone. Jesus's ministry in Mark's gospel looks as if it consumed a single explosive month. Before we know it, he is betrayed by his own followers, seized by a fickle crowd, brutalized by the Romans, and killed in the most horrific way imaginable. What happened next was a matter of significant debate among the early followers of this man and his perplexing movement. As the quote at the beginning of this Introduction testifies, Mark's way of telling the story can't help but leave us with questions.

John knew Mark's story, I believe, and that is the main reason he wrote in the way he did. John wrote his evangel in part to turn Mark's understanding of Jesus upside down and to replace Mark's tragedy with what seems at times to be almost a Christian farce. John insists on answers and unquestioning obedience. He does not like open-ended problems; he intends to tie things up, once and for all.

Here is how John managed it. In the most intense and shattering moment of Mark's gospel, Jesus separates himself from his followers and, when he is alone, prays in despair in a place called Gethsemane. He prays for God "to take this cup away from me," since he senses that his death is very near. God remains silent. Jesus is arrested, tortured, and then killed. His final cry from the cross ("My God, my God, why have you abandoned me?") is a pure cry of desperation and abandonment. John turns that story upside down by insisting that Gethsemane, as the Synoptic gospels all tell it, never happened. The evangel of John shows us a Jesus who actually makes fun of the Gethsemane prayer. And that is how Mark's tragedy was slowly turned into a comedy of Christian error. The tragedy for the history of later Christianity, especially in the Protestant era, is that John's heartless version of the gospel won out, leaving a corrupted skeleton of Christian compassion in its wake. It is that two-sided sad story, the one about Jesus and the one about John, that I wish to tie together and to tell.

What I will suggest in this book is rather simple, yet it is also deeply disturbing: the last of the four canonical gospels, John's evangel, represents a deliberate upending of the Christian world that Mark had done so much and so brilliantly to create. John's evangel paints the picture of a remarkably different Jesus. John's Jesus does not try to keep anything quiet. John's Jesus publicly suggests that he is equal to God, much to the outraged objection of most Jews and probably to the consternation of most Romans. John's Jesus had all the time in the world to keep repeating himself—his shocking ministry lasted three years or longer, according to John. Perhaps most important of all, John's Jesus never doubts anything. He knows that he has come to earth as God's equal and that at the end of his mission, he will be betrayed by the Jews and executed by the Romans. When the end is near, he never blinks. How could he, he smiles coldly, when this is the very thing he came to earth to do?

That is the shocking twist in John's new story: Jesus came to earth to die on a cross. This is a very powerful—and a very untragic—idea, and it has had a long life in subsequent Christian churches. Most Christians today probably still imagine Jesus in this way, which shows how successfully John's evangel has drowned out Mark's gospel and the other Synoptic versions. But the line that the earliest followers of Jesus were so very concerned to draw—the line that distinguishes a religious *martyrdom,* which is legitimate, from a reckless act of *suicide,* which is not—this is almost impossible to draw in John. John's Jesus looks very much like a suicide, if it is possible for a not so very human being to commit suicide. (And if Jesus was not human, then how can a human being ever hope to imitate him?) What John's views gradually did to the very texture of Christian compassion has often been deeply destructive and should be deeply troubling, if we take them seriously.

Of the four gospels in the New Testament, John's is the only one that is "evangelical," in the modern sense of that term, by design. At the end of his account, John says that if he had tried to write down everything Jesus said and did, then "all the books in the world could not contain them" (John 21:25). "But these things have been written," he notes, "so that you may believe . . . and in believing you may have life in his name forever" (John 20:30). It seems to me that John would have been most useful for people who had never heard the Christian story before; it is still the "gospel" of choice for new converts. Mark, by contrast, was writing to a community that already knew the story but needed to think about it in new ways to face new challenges. That difference in intended audience changes everything. John's Jesus offers food so that you will never be hungry again, water so that you will never be thirsty again, and a vision of a world in which no one who has faith will ever shed a tear.

Mark makes no such promises and reminds us of the opposite truth. Christians do go hungry. Christians do thirst.

Christians suffer and die, often unjustly, just like everyone else. For Mark, the point is that Christians witness suffering and death differently than other people do. They do so with *compassion,* a word that literally means "to suffer with." Mark's Jesus followers believed that God suffers with them. And one thing more, the crucial thing, the tragic thing: they believed that "salvation," as the German philosopher Hegel famously remarked in a letter, "is through suffering, not from it."[1] Mark's gospel presents us with an unblinking portrait of Jesus in pain, in spiritual as well as bodily pain. Mark's Jesus prays to God at the final hour, in Gethsemane, desperately wishing not to have to go through with it. Mark's Jesus, for all of his mystery, is also the patron saint of any subsequent Christian who has suffered compassionately, who has denied none of his or her doubt and pain and yet who has continued to hope in the face of bleakness and despair. I can think of no message more fitting or more timely for a triumphalist church that refuses to see the suffering around it, as well as the suffering it has inflicted on a bleeding world.

So there is an enormous conflict in the Bible, a conflict best symbolized by these two early Christian writers, Mark and John. That great divide, which is actually embedded in the very fabric of the New Testament, represents the most decisive conflict of all Christian conflicts, in my judgment, one that left its imprint indelibly on the tradition that Christianity was destined to become. Mark and John represent the fundamental fork in the early Christian road. That is the argument I will try to develop in this book. The traces of the conflict between these two men—their fingerprints, if you will—have been there all along in the scriptural clay, for anyone with eyes to see it. But excavations take time and patience and very careful attention.

Back to the Past

A final question comes into focus now: How is it that this howling conflict between Mark and John has not been noticed before? If the fingerprints have always been in the scriptural clay, then why haven't we seen them before? The short answer is that the conflict *was* apparent to the earliest Christians but that *modern* Christians have forgotten or ignored it. In the second and third centuries of the Christian era, many Christians already had problems with John. But there is another answer, a better answer, and this has to do with two of the most important archaeological discoveries in the history of New Testament studies.

Both discoveries occurred in the immediate aftermath of the Second World War. The first was the discovery of the so-called Dead Sea Scrolls in the cave-dwellings of Qumran, not far from the Dead Sea itself. These scrolls constitute a very large body of Jewish writings dating roughly from the first century B.C.E. They offer stunning evidence for how varied and conflicted Jewish identity was in the early years of the Roman occupation, in the generations before Jesus. Some Jews believed that with their kingdom now gone for good, the maintenance of God's law and special attention to the ritual activity at God's Temple in Jerusalem was the very essence of Jewish identity and religious duty. Others believed that the

Temple and its rituals and in fact the whole cult in Jerusalem were corrupt; they removed themselves literally and figuratively from Jerusalem and its Temple, preferring to live lives of purity in one of the most forbidding and inhospitable places on earth. Others felt that their Jewish duty was to resist, to fight the Romans and achieve their kingdom again. The point is that Jews of the time argued with one another about all the fundamentals of Judaism, so that when we see Jesus engaged in similar arguments in the gospels, he is not doing anything particularly new or different. The simple fact of all this Jewish argument is the key.

The second discovery involves the so-called Nag Hammadi Library, a discovery of twelve codices buried in ceramic jars in some nondescript caves in the Egyptian desert. These texts suggest the very same thing, but in Christian terms, not Jewish ones. These books are filled with alternative gospels, gospels associated with Judas and Thomas and Mary Magdalene, gospels that have been much in the news in recent years. The cumulative weight of what they say makes very clear that there was at least as much argument among Christians in the third century C.E. as there had been among Jews in Jesus's own day. Everywhere we turn, it seems, there is conflict and argument—even in the Jewish and Christian scriptures.

In short, these archaeological discoveries have sensitized us to the presence of religious conflict within scripture. Perhaps the best place with which to illustrate this point is in a famous passage where Luke describes the formation of a miraculous new kind of community in the wake of Jesus's final disappearance in Jerusalem. The community, Luke suggests, was organized around a radical new principle of selfless and reconciling love.

> The whole community of believers were of one heart and one soul, and no one called their property their own, but everything was held in common. With great power, the apostles gave witness to the rising of the Lord Jesus, and great grace was with them all. There was not a needy person among them, for as many as owned lands or houses sold them and laid the profits of what was sold at the apostles' feet. Then it was distributed to anyone who had need of it [Acts of the Apostles 4:32–35].

That was believed to be Luke's story, the surprisingly simple story of a love-inspired communism where each is given according to his or her need and where the apostles are in total agreement about what to preach and what to do. It is an idyllic world without argument or conflict or disagreement; everyone has the same heart and soul. Far too many Christians stop reading right there.

The trouble is, the very next story Luke tells (Acts 5:1–11) is the story of Ananias and his wife, Sapphira, who sell a piece of their own property and bring only some of the proceeds to the apostles. The remainder they presumably kept for themselves. Peter confronts Ananias with this deception, and he lies about it. So Peter condemns him, and he mysteriously drops dead. Then Sapphira is brought before Peter, not knowing what has just happened to her husband, and she repeats the same lie. So Peter repeats the same condemnation, and the punishment is repeated as well: she drops dead too. Not surprisingly, the real glue holding this community together now is fear (Acts 5:11). Everything is not sweetness and light and harmony in the early Christian community. Selfishness has not disappeared; nor has dishonesty; nor has the hungry grab for power among the leaders. Soon there will be conflict about matters of even greater moment, questions concerning who Jesus was and what his scandalous death meant. The arguments will intensify and move on to new subjects, such as whether Jews and Greeks can eat together, whether Greek converts need to be circumcised, whether Greek converts need to keep the laws of Moses, and so on.

What I am suggesting is that prior to the discovery of the Dead Sea and Nag Hammadi materials, Christians (especially Protestants, who identify most explicitly with what they call "the early Church") tended to recall the "sweetness and light" version of their own origins and simply failed to pay attention to all the conflict. When we notice the fingerprints left by all this apostolic meddling and argument, a very different picture of early Christian formation begins to emerge. And we just so happen to be in an ideal position to see it more clearly now. It is as if the sun has finally crested the hill, shedding new light on our excavations, so that the apostles' and evangelists' fingerprints may at long last receive their due.

CHAPTER ONE

In the Beginning . . .

The Modern Quest for Christian Origins

Tragedy is the form that promises us a happy ending. It is also the form
that is realistic about the matter.

—WALTER KERR, *TRAGEDY AND COMEDY* (1967)

When the Romans completed their long war against Mediterranean piracy, every renegade harbor on Crete lay in ruins. Phalasarna, where I worked for five years, was likely the pirates' last stand, since the Romans marched from the east, and when it fell, the war was effectively over. The destruction is hard to describe; when Romans intended to put an end to things, they put a period to their imperial sentences. They put a period to Phalasarna, too, so effectively that the site was never occupied again—at least until the impressive archaeological discoveries there created a tourist industry in its wake, and the pretty olive fields and grazing hills were handed over to Eurotourism. That's when the bright marble facades and new hotels commenced.

Before they left, Roman soldiers toppled the leading fortification towers into the mouth of the narrow entrance channel at Phalasarna, closing the harbor to all subsequent shipping. They burned or demolished the acropolis and all remaining battlements. They sowed salt into the soil so that nothing would grow. To this day, the little fishing harbor at Phalasarna lies on the opposite side of the great bay. The classical city was finished. And the task for Cretans in the next generation was to figure out how to start over, how to begin again.

Around the same time that Phalasarna fell, the Roman occupation of Palestine was nearing completion. Roman troops entered Jerusalem in the same decade that they finished off western Crete. What they could not have known at the time was how much trouble this Palestinian province would cause them. Revolutionary Jewish resentment simmered always just below the surface in Roman Palestine, and it boiled over twice into war (in 66–70 C.E. and again in 132–135), with horrific casualties and consequences. Jesus had been executed by the Roman civil administration in Palestine a generation before the first all-out war began. Whatever happened then, it is clear that he was executed by the Romans, not the Jews (Jewish religious courts did not have authority to render judgment in capital crimes under the Romans); hence he was likely executed as a political criminal and rabble-rouser. That is what execution by crucifixion symbolized in the outlying Roman provinces. As we now know, that event—the violent execution of the man his disciples "had hoped would save Israel"—represented a scandal that the first several generations of Jesus followers all felt the need to explain. Their strategies for doing so would vary, much as we might expect—from denying that it really happened, to denying that Jesus had a physical body for it to happen to, to the even more radical answer that Mark provided: namely, that tragic suffering represents the real, if rocky, road to redemption.

Thirty-some years after Jesus's execution, the province of Palestine erupted in revolt. The end result of four years of carnage was another systematic march over a region in rebellion, an even bloodier repetition of what the Romans did on Crete. The archaeological record suggests that this was the worst destruction the city of Jerusalem ever experienced in its long and tortured history. Even the Temple in Jerusalem, which the Romans themselves had paid to rebuild, was destroyed. In their first two generations, then, the earliest followers of Jesus endured two hammer blows, both at the hands of the Romans. Their leader was condemned and executed in the most shocking way imaginable; then their homeland and their capital were destroyed. The primary task for these people lay in figuring out how to move on, how to begin again. The answer to that question lay, in part, in the invention of a new literary genre: the gospel.

Between the time of Jesus's execution and the destruction of Jerusalem, stories about Jesus began circulating orally throughout the Greek-speaking eastern Mediterranean. (Some later Christians who believed that "the body is a temple" actually equated these two disasters, the destruction of Jesus and the destruction of the Temple.) In this same forty-year interim, some Jews who had followed Jesus became convinced, even after his scandalous death, that he was indeed the messiah, the one chosen to initiate a new covenantal relationship between God and Israel and (at least according to one understanding of what the prophets of Israel had predicted) everyone on earth. They took to the road shortly after the mysterious experience of Jesus's rising, scattered from the center in Jerusalem, traveled alone or in pairs and preached their various understandings of the meaning of what had happened by hanging it all on a story that began a very long time ago, with Abraham. There was no one to control the message as it spread.

Chaos ✱

These were tumultuous times of conflicting religious and political expectations, and although they met with only mixed success, these early preachers did meet with some, enough so that in the Syrian city of Antioch they began calling themselves "Christians" for the first time—although, as I have said, it is not entirely clear what this name meant to them. It meant at least this much: within a generation or two, some Jews and non-Jews had heard some version of Jesus's story and became convinced that it meant the beginning of a new world, even if what this world entailed was not entirely clear. Among such people, telling the stories of what Jesus had said, of what he had done, and of how he had died became an important part of their own devotional life. Eventually, the stories would be pieced together in a more comprehensive and far more dramatic way.

We can imagine that this all came about quite slowly, so haltingly, in fact, that this first generation of Christian bards and storytellers[1] had no idea of what was eventually to be invented in their names: a gospel. Just as few Greeks ever asked to hear the whole *Iliad* or *Odyssey* narrated at one sitting, few early Christians would have been accustomed to hearing an entire gospel at one sitting. They heard snippets—mysterious sayings,

Zen-like paradoxes, incredible stories of healing power. An astonishing variety of tales about what Jesus said and did were in circulation, with the emphasis, typical of all such storytelling, naturally focused on his pithiest sayings and his most dramatic miracles. These traditions, too, trickled out slowly over time; indeed, it took a very long time, forty years or more, for them to be assembled into a coherent story line by someone who chose a literary genre with which and through which to organize them. I will show this to be Mark's great achievement and hope to demonstrate that the new genre he created, the Christian gospel, was highly influenced by Greek tragedy. But all that lay a generation in the future. What happened immediately after Jesus's scandalous execution is where his followers' story actually began.

The Rising

Luke tells us the story in a memorable but rather confusing way. Immediately after Jesus's crucifixion, two men are walking together on the road leading out of the city of Jerusalem to a neighboring village called Emmaeus (Luke 24:13–49). One of these men seems to be a Jew with a Greek name, Cleopas;[2] the other man is never named. It was not a particularly long journey, roughly seven miles or so. The Romans still used the Greek length of a stade (which was roughly 200 meters, or one length of a Greek athletic *stadium,* hence the name). So when Luke says that they had to walk sixty stades,[3] he is also subtly reminding us that these men are culturally Greek and that they are running,

running away from Jerusalem. Luke tells us that the two had both been followers of Jesus, and now, just two days after his execution, they are leaving town. They are not leaving the city to take a break, and they are clearly not leaving town to begin preaching Jesus's message. Just the opposite, in fact. They have given up entirely. Jesus's mission, on which they had pinned all of their hopes, has ended in failure. His betrayal by a close friend with the help of a cadre of Jerusalem priests and his crucifixion by the Roman civil administration have created a scandal of which these two men wish simply to be free. It's time to go home, time to bind up old wounds, time to begin to forget.

Another man joins them on the way and asks what they are talking about. They respond as gossipy Greeks are wont to do: "Are you the only man in the entire city of Jerusalem who hasn't heard what happened over the past three days?" They mention Jesus of Nazareth, call him "a mighty prophet in word and deed," and then reiterate the scandal of his bitter ending. What they say next is especially haunting, poignant, and lovely. "We had hoped," they begin, "hoped that he was the one to save Israel" (Luke 24:21). Clearly, that hope is finished; after all, these men are leaving. And they are leaving despite the fact that earlier in the morning, several of the women who had accompanied Jesus to Jerusalem, all the way from Galilee, had gone to his tomb and found it empty. Everything is a mess; now their friend's tomb may have been desecrated. So these followers of Jesus are leaving, wishing to be free of this whole sad and sordid business.

The stranger berates them. He asks ironically how anyone can be so blind. And then he walks through the Hebrew scriptures with them, "starting with Moses and working through all the Prophets" (Luke 24:27). The stranger demonstrates that all of these things have happened according to a plan, a plan clearly laid out in the scriptures, one that insists paradoxically that the only path to glory is through suffering (what Luke calls *pathos*).

That is a lot of scripture to work through. By the time the stranger has finished, the group has arrived at the outskirts of Emmaeus. It is getting on toward evening, so Cleopas and his anonymous friend invite the stranger to stay with them. The man agrees. And as soon as they are seated at table together, "their eyes were opened" (Luke 24:31). They recognized the stranger as Jesus himself. And in that same moment, for reasons no one can explain, he vanishes. Only now do they begin talking excitedly with one another, remarking on how "their very heart had burned" when he was talking with them on the way. And so despite the lateness of the hour, they retrace their steps and return to Jerusalem. "We had hoped," they had remarked sadly, just a few hours earlier. Past tense. Now that hope has been reborn.

The two men return to a different city or at least to a very different circle of friends. Everything is in an uproar. A large group of women had returned to Jesus's graveside on the morning after the Sabbath; his tomb was empty, and two dazzling angels had informed them that he was no longer there, that he had "risen up," just as he had predicted he would in Galilee. This is interesting. The Jesus Luke describes in his gospel was always surrounded by women, so much so that some members of his audience were a bit shocked, if not scandalized (not only

Greeks love gossip, after all). Luke tells us who some of these women were by name: Mary of Magdala first; then an otherwise unknown woman named Joanna; then another woman named Mary, who is presumably Jesus's mother;[4] and an anonymous group of others. The women dutifully return to the disciples, the inner circle of Jesus's male followers, and report what they saw and heard at his tomb. No one believes them; we are not told why. Is it because they are women? Is it because the disciples cannot believe that they wouldn't be told first? Or is it that what they have reported, about Jesus' "rising up," is simply too much for them to believe? We don't know yet.

What we do know is that Jesus himself, or an apparition of him, has appeared to two men on the Emmaeus road. By the time these two get back to Jerusalem and rejoin the disciples, Jesus has struck again. Now he has appeared to Simon, the disciple he nicknamed Peter, "the Rock," and everyone has gathered together in a buzz of renewed excitement. The other shoe finally drops. Jesus appears again, to all of them gathered together. And here is the amazing thing: they are still afraid, and they still do not believe their eyes. They are afraid that he is a spirit or a ghost.[5] So Jesus puzzles it out patiently with them. "Look at me," he smiles reassuringly. "Does a spirit have flesh and blood as I do?" He "shows them his hands and feet" (Luke 24:39, though it's not clear what Luke means by that),[6] and still the group doesn't believe him. But the phrases Luke uses now are sympathetic, gracious, and reassuring. Jesus understands that now they doubt "out of joy and wonder" (Luke 24:41). They don't want to believe, they are actually afraid of believing, and so they deny what they are seeing with their own eyes.

So he proves his point by, well, by eating. For some reason, a little fish and bread seals it; they know it is Jesus, in the flesh, before them now. Eating had always been symbolically important to his ministry, according to Luke—what he ate and with whom.

Jesus now reiterates what he said on the road to Emmaeus. He uses the Hebrew scriptures to prove that there is a straight line leading from suffering to repentance (or "change of heart") to the release from sins. He tells his apostles that he intends for them to "preach"[7] this message to all peoples, beginning right here in Jerusalem. But not right away. Jesus tells them that first they must wait, in Jerusalem, until they are "clothed with a higher power" (Luke 24:49). Then they all walk to the outskirts of the city together, and Jesus disappears again. The elated group returns to the city, devoting each day to the ceaseless praise of God in the Jerusalem Temple.

This is a very strange and mysterious story, once we begin to think about the details. For starters, the nature of Jesus's resurrection, if that is what it was, is not clear at all. He seems more like a phantasm than a man, and it is interesting that this is the first impression the disciples have when they see him. He goes out of his way to prove his bodiliness to them, goes out of his way to eat and drink in front of them, but then he disappears. In fact, throughout the day, it seemed as if Jesus were more like a live wire: each time he touches the ground, there is an explosion, and he is blown some distance away by the blast. He is buried in Jerusalem. Then he is gone. Next he is walking on the road to Emmaeus. Then he is back in Jerusalem, with Peter. Then he appears to all of his followers together. Then he is gone for good.

25

First Questions

There is an important catch in Luke's story: the mystery and confusion about to whom Jesus appears and why. The first people to be alerted to the fact that something astonishing has happened are all women, although Jesus himself does not appear to them; two angels do. Jesus himself first appears to two otherwise nondescript followers, only one of whom is even named. Then and only then does he appear to his dear friend Simon Peter and then at last to the entire group of his closest followers and friends. How were they to interpret this? Is Jesus playing favorites? And if so, why *these* favorites, in *this* order, rather than the people whom he had favored during his lifetime? As we will see, the question of who knew what about Jesus and when they knew it will bear directly on who can claim authority in the life of the community as it tried to form itself in Jesus's absence. Who should be the leader of the community, with Jesus gone? Should it be Peter, of whom Jesus seemed especially fond in life? Should it be Jesus's family, at least two of whom, Mary and James, are right here in Jerusalem? (It is striking that neither his father nor his other brothers are mentioned.) Should it be Mary of Magdala, about whom we know very little in the canonical gospels, but whom Pope Gregory the Great turned into the very paradigm of the penitent whore in a famous homily he delivered in 591 (and whom a modern audience more inclined to sex and romance wants to turn into Jesus's lover and the mother of his children)? Or should it be Paul, who never met Jesus when he was alive but who will shortly receive an important visit (Acts 9:1–19) from this risen mystery-man himself? It is not just the world which Jesus's rising has turned upside down; his community of closest followers has been totally disrupted as well. Now they must try to pick up the pieces, reassemble their broken following, and come to terms with the lingering scandal of Jesus's execution.

The two men on the road to Emmaeus had hoped that Jesus was the one, and their hope had been shattered. Yet Luke's gospel ends with a deliberately mysterious story of how their hope was restored. How was it restored? What did Cleopas and his friend mean by "save" when they said, "We had hoped that he was the one who would save Israel"?

The answer to that question may be found in the first chapter of Luke's second volume of "Christian" history, the Acts of the Apostles, which purports to be the record of how this first generation of Jesus's followers formed their community in his absence. Apparently, Jesus did not disappear forever on the day he left his followers outside of Jerusalem, near Bethany. Rather—and this idea will recur in many of the noncanonical gospels found at Nag Hammadi in Egypt, as we shall see—he appeared periodically to them for the next forty days, discussing the Kingdom of God with his disciples and answering all of their questions. He also insisted that they should wait in Jerusalem, not leaving until they have been rebaptized with "holy spirit," as they had previously been baptized with water. Now we come to the heart of the issue that Luke's story raises; many of the noncanonical gospels raise it as well: given the chance to ask Jesus one last question, what would yours be?

If a modern person were given an opportunity to ask Jesus one question before he departed, I suspect that it would take the following form. "What happens to us when we die?" "Will I be reunited with my mother, my father, my children, my lover, my friends?" "What did you mean when you said such-and-such?" "Is hell a real place?" or "What does God's love mean, and is it anything like the love of which I am capable?" Such questions come quite naturally to modern and more literate Christian minds. What is remarkable is that no such questions came to Jesus's disciples.

No, they speak with one voice, according to Luke; there is only one question on their minds: "Lord, will you now, in this time, restore the Kingdom of Israel?" (Acts 1:6). That, apparently is what they meant by "save." Saving Israel means restoring the kingdom of David and Solomon, an independent kingdom that presumably could only be restored when they kicked the Romans out. That is the question on their minds; it is a question about politics and history. Only now are we in a position to realize that Jesus, for forty long days, has been telling them about the Kingdom of God, insisting that it is not the same sort of kingdom as Rome's or Greece's or Israel's. Then the mystery deepens. Jesus does not tell them that questions about kingdoms are wrong or that they should stop asking them. He simply refuses to answer. What he says is that God has a timetable for things like that and that their job is different now. They are to wait—all of this interminable waiting in the gospels!—and once "holy spirit" has come to them, then they will preach, "to the very end of the earth" (Acts 1:8). This time Jesus really is gone for good. So Peter takes up informal leadership of the community and suggests that they appoint a new apostle named Matthias to replace Judas, the betrayer, who has been killed in the interim (Acts 1:15–26). And thus ten days after Jesus's final disappearance (*Pentecost* literally refers to the "fifty days" that have passed since the Passover, in Greek), something called "holy spirit" descends on the apostles in a gust of Jerusalem wind (Acts 2:1–47), and the grand adventure of turning this local Jerusalem sect into a global Greek religion began.

First Arguments

Several important things come into sharper focus when we read the New Testament with a critical eye aimed at what archaeologists and historians can help us see. They help us see the human fingerprints of these authors and the communities that produced them. Archaeologists have discovered scores of other gospels and gospel fragments, most of them buried in the desert sands and hidden caves of Egypt. These discoveries have dramatically altered our understanding of how religious communities form in the first place.

Such communities are formed, of course, by human beings. And those human beings, predictably enough, argue about what the best form of religious community should be, who should lead it, whether it should have rules, and if so, what kinds of rules and designed by whom. One of the most distinguishing features of the early "Christian" landscape is the way in which these people tried to get away from the language of rules and laws. Something they began calling "the gospel," they believed, had trumped "the law"—and when they spoke of the Law, they meant the Law of Moses, as found in the

Torah, the first five books of the Hebrew Bible. Some followers of Jesus seemed to believe that Christianity called for a kind of anarchism or lawlessness (I'll have more to say about these Christian mavericks later on). Others insisted that this new faith required a radicalization of the laws found in the Torah and in the familiar political structure of the Roman Empire. They felt that they had been called to a kind of moral perfection. Still others felt that the language of "law" needed to go but that Jesus followers should still have a "short list" of proper and forbidden behavior. There are sayings and doings of Jesus recorded in the canonical gospels that clearly reflect each of the three positions I have just outlined. In short, many of the early Jesus followers believed that Jesus thought just as they did and that his sayings confirmed what they themselves believed. But the trick is, these same communities began circulating gospels designed to confirm their own beliefs, essentially making Jesus say what they thought he should have said. So far as we know, Jesus himself never wrote a word.

As I emphasized in the Introduction, for all of its focus on *agape,* the unique qualities of reconciling Christian love, the New Testament is actually riddled with conflict, arguments about things that matter by people who believed that they mattered enough to get them exactly right. The New Testament may be a collection of books aiming at love, but its writers argued about the distinguishing features of that love and about who best embodied that love. Followers of Jesus argued about who had authority and what the nature of true religious authority was, as well as about the proper extent of human behavior for which such authority figures were appropriate judges. In short, religious traditions are often best understood as arguments extended through time about matters of special significance to their practitioners. Traditions are always partly defined by the arguments they have about themselves, and scriptures are often the repositories that record the results of these debates.

One of the reasons that there are so many gospels is that every early community of Jesus followers apparently felt authorized to write one. And what they wrote was an attempt to depict their own understanding of the answers to these absolutely fundamental questions about proper religious authority, right religious rules, and the Christian quality of human life. The fingerprints and other marks left by these conflicts are still visible in the scriptural clay of the New Testament, if we are careful enough to look for them.

We know that the first followers of Jesus argued ferociously with one another about whether Greeks and Romans should be allowed into their communities (Acts 10:1–11:20). We also know that these same Jesus followers argued about whether Greek converts needed to be circumcised or to adopt the Law of Moses (Acts 15:1–35). We know that Paul argued very publicly with Peter over these very questions, and essentially called him a hypocrite (Galatians 2:11–16), which was a heavy charge for any follower of Jesus to bear, since Jesus came down especially hard on religious hypocrisy in so many of his Synoptic sayings. We know that Jesus's family, especially his brothers (and maybe his mother), had a sort of authority different from the kind his other followers and friends had.[8] And we also catch the fleeting sense that to some early followers of Jesus, Mary of Magdala was deemed to have an authority that was altogether unique, given the amount of time she shared with Jesus in private conversation. I'll return to this point as well.

First Answers

Two enormous questions followed for Jesus's followers after his execution, rising, and the Pentecost. The first was political. What about the Romans? What about the kingdom of Israel? Was it time to rise up in a messianic revolt? The second question was metaphysical. Who was he? Who exactly was Jesus, given how much of what he did and said and what happened to him remains a mystery? Within two generations of Jesus's death and the formation of the first nominally Christian communities, a remarkably creative strategy was developed for answering both of these questions—and for tying them together. A man named Mark invented a new literary genre, one that he called an *evangelion* (Mark 1:1), which we translate into English as a *gospel*. In Mark's gospel, the political and the metaphysical questions are brilliantly combined. In fact, Christian gospels are designed to answer two simple but far-reaching questions: Who was he? and Why did he die that way?

Mark did this fully one generation after Jesus's execution, dramatic rising, and eventual disappearance. With most of the eyewitnesses to these events now dead or dying, Mark preserved the memory of these events in part by inventing a new genre, the Christian gospel, weaving together these traditions about the remarkable sayings and great doings of Jesus into a powerful tragedy that culminated in his Passion, death, and disappearance. Mark's gospel was also crafted in such a way as to raise a number of questions that Mark's distinctly tragic manner of presentation makes impossible to answer clearly. Jesus was only active for a month; there was never enough time to make things clearer. Furthermore, there were many matters of importance that Jesus did not wish to make clear: the fact of his own messianic status primarily, which he apparently wished to keep secret.[9] He taught in parables in order to confuse matters still further (Mark 4:1–12). And when he finally did speak clearly, no one, not even his disciples, took his point. Small wonder that they all failed him in the end.

Over the course of the next fifteen years (70–85 C.E.), Matthew's and Luke's versions of Mark's tragic gospel endeavored to answer some of the questions that Mark's presentation left most opaque and incomprehensible. They tried to clarify a great deal of what remained unclear in Mark's version of the gospel. Jesus's status as the messiah, or Christ, was clarified and explained more clearly to his followers. Many, if not most, of the parables were explained; new parables were reported that helped illuminate the older ones. And as we will see in the next chapter, the failure of the disciples to stand by Jesus in the garden of Gethsemane had less to do with fate or lack of knowledge and more to do with weakness of the will.

Luke clearly modeled what he did on Mark's gospel, however much he added to it and even changed it along the way; Matthew did much the same thing. That's an important detail to remember. The record of how Jesus's followers came to terms with his rising was written down one or two generations later by men who knew many things that the apostles themselves could not have known. Here is the crucial point: the people we meet *in* the New Testament *did not have* a New Testament. The only Bible they had was the Hebrew Bible or, rather, a Greek translation of that Bible known as the Septuagint.[10]

What I have laid out in Luke's story of Jesus's rising and its aftermath emphasizes what is most stirring and powerful— and tragic. The fact that God's chosen prophet and Son could have died in such a scandalous way, abandoned even by his own closest followers, and executed like a common crimi- nal by the Romans—that was a hard pill for the disciples to swallow. It still is. The biblical God is supposed to be stead- fast, and faith in such a God is supposed to be rewarded. Faith and its rewards—such is the stuff of most Christian sermons even today. And yet, as Paul emphasized in several of his more famous letters, the very heartbeat of Jesus Christ's story is his crucifixion, an event Paul already referred to as a "scan- dal."[11] This is a telling detail, because the letters in the New Testament are the oldest "Christian" material we have, written fifteen years or more *before* Mark wrote down his gospel and thus the earliest written evidence we have for what some fol- lowers of Jesus said and believed. The point is that the Synoptic gospel writers already knew that the crucifixion was a "scan- dal." That is the fundamental Christian truth that John was intent on changing.

So fifteen to twenty years later (90–100 C.E.), with every eyewitness dead, and most likely after Mark's own demise, John chose to compose his own version of events. John, as we will see, had a very different conception of what a gospel ought to be. That is why I refer to his creation as an *evangel* rather than a gospel. Perhaps John knew the Synoptic gospels; perhaps he did not (scholars have made strong arguments for both possibilities). But this much is certain: John's evangel has a very different chronology than Mark's gospel does, boasting a three-year public ministry. John's Jesus does not teach in parables the way Mark's does, and perhaps the most memorable speech in Matthew's and Luke's gospels, the so-called Sermon on the Mount (or Plain), is also absent. A host of mystifying "I am" sayings takes the place of the Synoptic parables, and most of them would have created an obvious scandal, according to the religious scruples of first-century Judaism. Finally, and this is so important that I will devote the next chapter to it, John's gospel ends with Jesus's mocking rejection of the prayer in Gethsemane and an oddly described, virtually *triumphant* death on a cross.

More than two Christian roads diverged after Jesus's death and rising, to be sure, but these two paths proved to be determinative. Death or new life? Agony or triumph? Benediction or bloodbath—or both? Should we turn to Mark's gospel or John's evangel for wisdom and discernment? Mark's gospel attempted to make *tragic* sense of who Jesus was and how he died. Modern Christian churches have had a very hard time hanging on to the sober form of hope Mark recommends by emphasizing the apparent scandal of Jesus's doubt and divine abandonment. In Mark's hardened but deeply compassionate hands, none of what has happened makes faith impossible, nor is Christian hope disqualified. Rather, for Mark, suffering is simply the marrow of the only story worth telling, a story that really might change the world by altering our perspective on suffering and pain and compassion. He offers us a *tragic* hope that he believes may be able to withstand the tests of temptation and of time. The way to new life takes us through death—there is no gain without a commensurate loss—and it is only through the loneliness of Gethsemane that Christ came into his Kingdom. All human expectations are turned upside-down. And Mark reminds us that this turnabout is never easy—not for Jesus, not for his disciples, and certainly not for us, who are still attempting to listen to this story. Mark's gospel insists that it takes a tragedy to inspire the most power-ful tragic emotions, like pity, fear, and compassion. The heart of this tragic gospel is Jesus's agonized prayer in Gethsemane, his desire to avoid this kind of death. The irony of later Christian history is that when John rejected tragedy as a genre, and the description of Gethsemane as a prayer garden, and pity as an emotion compatible with salvation, then he unwittingly cut the heart out of Christian compassion. All that was left was fear.

CHAPTER TWO

The Heart of Christian Compassion

The Prayer in Gethsemane

For those on the outside everything is in parables, so that "looking they may not see, and listening they may not hear, lest they should turn around and be forgiven."

—MARK 4:10–12

Jesus said to him, "I am the way, and the truth, and the life. No one comes to the father except by me."

—JOHN 14:6

What I am imagining always takes place in front of a fire; I'm not quite sure why. It's got something to do with cool, late-evening breezes dancing across faces in silhouette, a stark contrast to the soothing internal warmth of fire, the calm decrescendo after a meal, that magical time when human thought turns most naturally to talk. I do not pretend that this meeting around a fire ever actually took place. For clarity's sake, I am simply taking on the role of a Christian storyteller, for a moment, and simply to make a point. Stories are not quite the same things as arguments, I know, but for some issues, they have real powers of elucidation. This is one such time, since what I am trying to imagine is the mysterious process of the development of Christian storytelling about Jesus, in the beginning.

Three visitors have come to a small town to tell a story that many of the locals have already heard, in bits and pieces, before: the story of Jesus, the son of Joseph, who may have hailed from Nazareth (or maybe it was Bethlehem)[1] and who was eventually recognized as God's anointed messiah. But there is a wrinkle; there is always one great wrinkle in this story. Jesus was betrayed by one of his own closest followers, abandoned by the rest, arrested by a hostile Jerusalem crowd (not all of them Jewish), and then put to death by the Romans. And there is also a rumor. There is a rumor that on the night of his betrayal, Jesus was tempted, and then he prayed, prayed to God to be delivered from all of this. Have these traveling "Christian" visitors heard *this* story? Of course, they have. Would they be interested in sharing what they have heard about it? Naturally—that's a large part of how these people "preach."

What I propose to do in this chapter is to examine in closer detail each of the four versions of the Gethsemane story as they now appear in the New Testament. As I have explained, there is not one Christian gospel; there are four very different gospels in the New Testament (as well as a host of other noncanonical versions that have been recovered in the past hundred years or so, most of them from Egypt). In many cases, and most definitely here, the subtle differences between the various gospel versions provide important clues as to what each writer thought his particular gospel was ultimately about. The distinctive fingerprints of these four writers are most clearly in evidence in the way they describe Jesus's Gethsemane prayer. Let me offer a few words of clarification before we begin.

First, the stories I relate here may have a slightly odd ring to them. That is in part because I have translated them myself. And in so doing, for the sake of emphasis, I will translate the common Greek term *mathetes* as "student" and then shift to the more common term "disciple" in my discussion of these stories. My intention is to help us keep in mind is that Jesus was clearly depicted as a teacher, a rabbi, in the Synoptic gospels[2] and that his students were "learners," at least until they were "sent out" (which is what "apostle," *apostoloi,* actually means in Greek) on their own. This is a perennial life-and-spirit pattern, after all: from student, to disciple, to adult authority out on your own.

Second, I may seem to be telling the stories out of order. Why do I begin with Luke's version of the story? As I trust is clear by now, Luke's version of some important Christian events has become "canonical" for most modern Christians in North America. His version of Christmas, with its dramatic story of Caesar's census and watchful Judean shepherds[3] (Luke 2:1–20), is the one most commonly celebrated by Christians each December, just after the winter solstice. His version of Jesus's mysterious rising (Luke 24:1–53) left a lasting mark on all subsequent Christian commemorations, as I noted in Chapter One. His definition of an "apostle" seems to have become vaguely official (Acts of the Apostles 1:21–22), and his version of the historical development of the earliest Christian churches (in Acts of the Apostles) is the only version of this history we have in the New Testament. As I hope to show in this chapter, Luke's version of Jesus's Gethsemane prayer, precisely because it is so artful and so eloquent, has also become vaguely canonical, and this fact has made it harder for us to hear the raw power and the tragic novelty of Mark's earlier version. So we will need to look briefly at Luke and Matthew first in order to perceive the Christian battle lines that were later drawn between Mark and John. Sometimes, as Jeffrey Stout reminds us, you must travel a great distance out of your way in order to go a short distance well.[4]

Here, then, is what I imagine was said in front of that long-ago Christian fireside—the various retellings of Luke and Matthew and Mark and John's decision to outdo, and undo, them all. It is a bit shocking to notice how different their stories really are.

Luke's Story

The first to offer to tell the tale is a Greek-speaking foreigner named Luke. He's remarkably cultivated and polite. The word on him is that he never actually met Jesus (he seems too young for that), but he knew and traveled extensively with Paul, a renegade quasi-apostle who never met Jesus personally either, but who claimed an authority for himself that was equal to that of those who knew Jesus best. That seems like an awfully large claim for a man as modest and peaceable as Luke seems to be. Clearly, he's learned as much as he can from everyone

[handwritten margin note: Paul never met Jesus.]

else who knew Jesus personally, and he's read all the ancient Greek and Jewish classics. He's really half a historian and half a poet at heart. "I love to hear this story almost as much as I love to tell it," he smiles reassuringly. "I'll go first, just to get us started. I'll tell you how others told the story to me but I'll put it together in my own way, with a poetic turn or two. I think you'll like it."

And he went out, as was his custom, to the Mount of Olives; and the students followed him. And when he came to the place, he said to them, "Pray that you may not enter into temptation." And he himself went off from them about a stone's throw, knelt down, and prayed, saying, *"Father, if you will, take this cup away from me. Still, let not my will be done, but yours."*

[Then an angel from heaven was seen with him, strengthening him. And his agony intensified as he prayed, and his sweat fell like drops of blood to the ground.][5]

Then he got up from prayer, came to his students and found them sleeping, far from sorrow, and he asked them, "Why are you sleeping? Get up and pray that you may not enter into temptation."

While he was still talking—behold, a crowd—and the one called Judas, one of the Twelve, went before them, and he drew near to Jesus to kiss him. But Jesus said to him, "Judas, are you betraying the Son of Man with a kiss?" And when those who were with him saw what was about to happen, they asked, "Lord, should we strike with a sword?" And one of them struck the high priest's slave and cut off his right ear.

In response, Jesus said, "Stop it!" And he touched the ear and healed it.

Then Jesus said to those who had surrounded him, the high priest and the officers of the temple and the elders, "Have you come out against me like a criminal, with swords and clubs? Every day I was with you in the temple and you did not lay hands on me. Still, this hour is yours, and the power of darkness" [Luke 22:39–53].

I have referred several times to the Gethsemane *prayer,* as well as to the fact that the Gethsemane story has fundamentally to do with temptation, prayer, and betrayal. This is a very Luke-inspired way of remembering things. In fact, Luke never even calls the place Gethsemane; only Mark and Matthew do that. What Luke does is to focus our attention on this late-night garden as a place of anguished prayer.

Luke was obsessed with prayer. Luke's Jesus, and only Luke's Jesus, is carefully and constantly portrayed as a praying Savior. Luke uses different forms of the Greek words for prayer and praying nearly three times as often as any of the other canonical storytellers. His obsession with praying is especially evident here on the Mount of Olives: some form of the word appears four times in five verses (five times in seven verses, if we include the controversial verses at Luke 22:43–45).[6] To anyone who has heard Luke's version of the story, it will be impossible not to focus on what Jesus prays and how. The heart of the matter is that the *way* we pray matters.

Luke's is far and away the sparest of the three Synoptic performances, although he is the most fluent in Greek. He artfully maximizes the impact he gets out of fewer words, like any good poet. He also seasons his story with an extraordinary wealth of classical Greek allusions, most of them from Homer and Greek tragedy. In Luke's telling, the story of Gethsemane is also a story about how you meet your fate, and he combines this with what we know are his main obsessions: following and prayer.

Luke alone tells us that Jesus went out to the Mount of Olives, as it was his custom to do, and that the disciples followed him there. In the other Synoptic performances, the disciples are "with Jesus," but no mention is made of the fact that they are "following." Luke thinks of obedient following as the very heart of Christian discipleship, and he wants to emphasize that the disciples ultimately failed to follow Jesus here. That is why, when they get to the Mount of Olives, Luke's Jesus issues a solemn injunction to his disciples, linking prayer to something else: temptation. "Pray," he warns them, "pray that you may not enter into temptation." This unexpected warning is never explained. What temptation is Jesus talking about? Exactly what is he expecting to happen? And why here? Why now?

The Greek terms *peira* and *peirasmon* are widely used throughout the New Testament,[7] but they seem to be fairly generic terms. "Temptation" is probably a good translation, since we may be tempted by many things, from a tempting slice of chocolate cake to a beautiful body or a beautiful soul. "Temptation" also implies more serious emotional states, ranging from passionate sexual desire to murderous rage. Apart from these vaguely moral meanings, there is also "a distinctly religious understanding of the concept."[8] The great religious temptation that underwrites all the others is the temptation to disobey or deny God. Confronted with temptation, you can surrender completely to God, you can rebel, or you can try to find a way to split the difference. Luke surrenders, Matthew splits the difference, and Mark rebels. John simply can't accept any of that.

Luke's performance of the Gethsemane prayer links following, prayer, and temptation in a very artful way. The temptation applies to Jesus and to his disciples alike. Harsh choices will be demanded of everyone very soon. God's way seems to involve arrest, abandonment, and death. The temptation to disobey God's mysterious will is greatest tonight. In Luke's story, Jesus seems to understand what is about to take place, as his closest followers clearly do not. They are literally and figuratively asleep.

So Jesus removes himself, "about a stone's throw," and prays that *he* may not be led into temptation. Luke's Jesus prays in a way that is unique to this gospel version: "Father, *if you will,* take this cup away from me." In no other gospel does Jesus ever pray like that.

If we pay close attention to the fingerprints in Luke's version, the way he imagines this story, we catch a clue about what he thinks this story is fundamentally about. As this small band of itinerants wander about on the Mount of Olives—as they have long been in the habit of doing—Jesus's warning about some imminent temptation must seem like the proverbial sailor's warning while the sky is blue. Their confusion increases when Jesus immediately sets himself apart, offering no explanation of what temptation he has in mind. Should they fear food or drink or fire? Next, we see what Jesus's disciples do not see—namely, exactly *how* they are supposed to pray. Jesus prays that he, too, may escape the test of temptation and by implication that he may be empowered to accept a will decidedly at odds with his own. Not only is this the only gospel performance that begins by mentioning "the will," but Luke also suggests that God's will and Jesus's will are radically at odds. And Luke—fatalist as he sometimes seems to be[9]—seems to be trying to imagine a world in which God's will is *everything*. That is why, if it is God's will that Jesus be killed, Luke does not ask why, as Mark does. Luke turns instead to prayer so that he may follow and submit.

We know that Jesus has prayed and that his disciples have not. We also know that his prayer had something to do with bringing his will in line with God's. Thus Jesus is now equipped to deal with the crisis that is brewing as his disciples will never be (at least not until Pentecost and their clothing in "holy spirit"). For Luke, the *anticipation* of suffering gives us the strength to endure it. *Prayer* is his word for when and how this happens. His audience, schooled as Luke was on Greek drama, would find this thought familiar. For Jesus, as opposed to his dozing disciples, the crisis will not come by surprise. This is Luke's main point in Gethsemane: honest anticipation makes us resolute. Our own wills are transformed by God's will, if not actually lost in it. Prayer is what triggers the change. Prayer is the only true armor against temptation. From this moment on, the distance between Jesus and the disciples steadily increases. If he was physically a stone's throw away, he has moved miles beyond them spiritually, and his character will continue to be on the rise, even as human events conspire against him Following, praying, temptation— the disciples fail every test.

Events move quickly in this short story. While Jesus is still speaking, the crowd approaches with Judas in the lead. He draws near to kiss Jesus but seems to be prevented from doing so. Only Matthew and Mark provide the background information necessary for this scene to make sense (it would be very difficult to read or to hear Luke's gospel all by itself). Judas has told the chief priests and elders that the man he kisses will be the one they seek (how could they not already know who he is?). In Luke, we have none of this explanation; instead, Jesus knows what no one else seems to know. Jesus equates the kiss with betrayal, asking and explaining all at once with a single question: "Judas, would you betray the Son of Man with a kiss?" (Luke 22:48).

The crowd of followers, which has dwindled, rallies one last time to Jesus's defense. "Lord, shall we strike with the sword?" (Luke 22:49). Before Jesus can answer, someone from the crowd answers his own question, cutting off the right ear of the chief priest's slave. Jesus responds curtly, "Stop it!" (Luke 22:51), and immediately he heals the slave's ear. In Luke's gospel, Jesus is regularly called upon to undo the damage other people do. Jesus then ironically interrogates the crowd and concludes with a strange observation: "This hour is yours, and the power of darkness." This conception of the power of darkness, and the wisdom of yielding to it, comes right out of Homer.[10] And in this fatal darkness, Jesus is spirited away.

Such are the harsh necessities of Luke's version of events. For unknown reasons, God does not wish to take this suffering cup away. By emphasizing prayer and the will, Luke offers us his explanation of what is happening. This is the tragic crisis in Jesus's life and ministry. Prayer creates the possibility of heroic

46

resolve. When God's will is accepted, then *our* will tends to disappear. Jesus's last words in Luke's gospel confirm this: "Father, I place my spirit in your hands" (Luke 23:46).[11]

This is a somewhat shocking conclusion, if you think about it. Mark thought about it a great deal and refused to believe it; John, by contrast, will actually exploit the idea and raise it to even greater rhetorical and theological heights. In John's version, Jesus's will does not need to disappear, because it is already one with God's and always has been, from the beginning of Creation.

But in Luke's story, the spotlight is on Jesus and Jesus alone. He has somehow managed to remain the commanding presence even in the course of his own betrayal: he prevents Judas from kissing him, he alone understands the signs of the times, he undoes the misplaced violence of his friends, and he voluntarily submits to the hour and its power. In the end, Jesus becomes the rather untragic hero in this strange story, the primary and indeed the only actor before whom all other characters—even the disciple who betrays him, and the crowd that condemns him—serve merely as a dramatic backdrop. Luke's Jesus escapes the worst of things by escaping into prayer and thus, in a mysterious way, by disappearing into God.

Matthew's Story

Next, a Jewish scribe from the region around Galilee named Matthew comes to the center of the circle. There is a rumor that he was one of the first people Jesus ever asked to join him and that he gave up a lucrative position with the Roman civil service to do just that. He's not quite as calm or as peaceful as Luke is; he seems to be working awfully hard just to keep it down, and he seems to snap every now and then when his story gets exciting. "I've spent my entire adult life on this story," he brags, "but it's a very difficult story to tell well." He clearly thinks his is the story to end all Jewish stories. And for a man who spoke briefly, his story lasted long.

Then Jesus went with them into the region called Gethsemane, and he told his students, "Sit here, while I go over there to pray." Then taking aside Peter and the two sons of Zebedee, he became sorrowful and distressed. And he told them, "My soul is very sorrowful until death. Stay here and watch with me." And when he went ahead a little further, he fell upon his face, praying, *"My Father, if it is possible, then let this cup pass me by. Still, not how I want it, but how you do."* Then he went back to his students and found them sleeping, and he said to Peter, "Are you not strong enough to watch for one hour with me? Watch and pray that you may not enter into temptation. The spirit is willing, but flesh is weak." Then again, a second time, he went away and prayed, saying, *"My Father, if it is not possible that this pass me by unless I drink it, then let your will be done."* And when he came again, he found them sleeping, for their eyes were heavy. So he left them, and he went away again, and he prayed a third time, saying the same thing. Then he returned to the students and said to them, "Are you still sleeping and resting? Behold, the hour has come, and the Son of Man is betrayed into the hands of sinners. Get up; let's go. Behold, the betrayer has come for me."

And while he was still speaking, behold, Judas, one of the Twelve, came, and with him a great crowd with swords and clubs from the high priests and elders of the people. Now the betrayer had given them a sign, saying, "He whom I kiss will be the man; seize him." And immediately he went up to Jesus and said, "Hello, Rabbi," and he kissed him. But Jesus said to him, "My friend, has it come to this?"

Then those who drew near laid hands upon Jesus and seized him. And behold, one of those with Jesus raised his hand, drew a sword, and struck the slave of the high priest and cut off his ear. Then Jesus said to him, "Return your sword to its place, for all who take up the sword will die by the sword. Do you suppose it is impossible for me to call upon my Father, who would immediately send me more than twelve legions of angels? But then how could the scriptures be fulfilled, that it must happen this way?" At the same time, Jesus said to the crowd, "Have you come out to seize me like a criminal with swords and clubs? Every day I sat in the temple teaching and you did not seize me. This has all happened in order that the writings of the prophets might be fulfilled." Then all the students left him and fled [Matthew 26:36–56].

Luke's version of the Gethsemane prayer is the main reason we call it the story of a prayer. The place where Jesus prays was the place where Jesus regained control of a situation and his own emotional state after they had both been threatened (or, in Luke's words, tempted). Matthew's story has less to do with prayer, and more to do with possibility. And what is strangest about Matthew's portrait of Jesus is that he seems to be a mysterious figure who is almost torn in two.

49

One of the most famous of all lines in Matthews's gospel is one he took from Mark, because it helps paint this picture best: "The spirit is willing, but flesh is weak" (Matthew 26:41, Mark 14:38). That is precisely how Matthew imagines Jesus in Gethsemane.

Matthew sets his performance, the longest of the four, in a place with a name—Gethsemane—an important detail that he also took from Mark. Matthew's performance shares a great deal of Mark's pathos and intensity too, as we will see. Jesus instructs his disciples to sit down while he goes off alone to pray. Having said this, presumably to all of the disciples, Jesus takes aside his inner circle of his three favorites ("Peter and the two sons of Zebedee"; Matthew 26:37), and with them alone, he begins to agonize in private—much as we saw in Luke's version. Jesus rather uncharacteristically tells them about his inner state of mind rather than merely showing it, as Luke did: "My soul is very sorrowful until death," he confesses. "Stay here and watch with me" (Matthew 26:38). This sorrow is the very thing to which Luke tells us the disciples were most oblivious. In Luke's story, they slept, "far from sorrow." Here Jesus himself tells the disciples about his sorrow, twice, and yet still they go to sleep. Jesus leaves even his three closest friends behind, tells them to keep watch, and goes on a little further to pray: "My Father, *if it is possible,* let this cup pass me by. Still, not how I want it, but how you do" (Matthew 26:39). The disciples, of course, are not watching because they are asleep. Jesus responds specifically to Peter, but his accusation is addressed in the plural, to the whole group. "Were you not strong enough to watch one hour with me?" (Matthew 26:40).

The repeated emphasis on one little phrase, "with me," is a wonderful stylistic turn, subtly directing our attention to Jesus's awful abandonment and loneliness. Matthew's story highlights the pathos of Gethsemane in a very different way than Luke's did. Jesus's loneliness is ironically increased by his disciples' very presence. He would probably feel less alone, and surely less abandoned, without them there. A sleeping friend is cold comfort to the person in pain. So Jesus intensifies his warning: "Watch and pray that you may not enter into temptation. The spirit is willing, but flesh is weak" (Matthew 26:41).

What is most striking about this passage is the way the concluding warning about willing spirit and weak flesh sticks to Jesus, too. "My soul is very sorrowful until death," he has just told his friends. John, as we will see, sneers at any such wavering portrait of Jesus. Though prayer may serve the same purpose for Matthew as it did for Luke, in Matthew's Gethsemane story, Jesus's anticipation seems far less resolute, somehow.

This is clearest when we notice that Matthew's Jesus prays not once but twice. No resolute divine soul would pray this way, but a divided *human* soul certainly might. Human souls are often torn in two—as Jesus is here. Matthew even reports the prayer twice. In general outline, the prayers match up, but they are decidedly not the same prayer. In fact, the subtle differences between the two are designed to show us Jesus's far more gradual reconciliation to the will of his Father, a resoluteness that is slowly and painfully earned, not simply anticipated. We may see this more clearly if we place the two prayers in parallel:

(v. 39)	(v. 42)
My Father,	My Father,
if it is possible,	if it is not possible
let this cup pass me by.	that this pass me by unless I drink it,
Still, not how I want it,	then let your will
but how you do.	be done.

Whereas Jesus's first prayer wonders what is possible, his second prayer assumes that it is *not* possible for the cup to pass unless he drinks it. In the conclusion to this second prayer, all mention of Jesus's will has disappeared.[12] This would seem to confirm the sense in which Jesus's prayers are presented as models by Matthew—prayers that disciples and other recipients of this story ought to pray as well.

It is in showing Jesus's response to the eruption of violence in the crowd that Matthew's performance is most distinctive and actually most strange. Jesus tells an anonymous follower to sheathe his sword, "for all who take up the sword will die by the sword" (Matthew 26:53). He then adds a bizarre afterthought: "Do you suppose it is impossible for me to call upon my Father, who would immediately send me more than twelve legions of angels? But then how could the scriptures be fulfilled, that it must happen this way?" (Matthew 26:53–54). Three points bear mentioning here. First, Jesus does not explicitly reject the use of violence; his reply presupposes the existence of "legions" (the Roman term for armies), even in heaven. Second, the comment makes nonsense of the very prayer Jesus has just offered up in

Gethsemane. After all, Jesus has just been praying for deliverance and concluded that it was not possible. Where, then, are God's legions? Third, and this is very different from Luke's version, Jesus finally explains why "it is not possible" for God to take this cup away. The scriptures must be fulfilled, he says, and can presumably be fulfilled in no other way. This point is reiterated, lest we miss it, two verses later when Jesus affirms it once again: "This has all happened in order that the writings of the prophets might be fulfilled" (Matthew 26:56). Matthew never tires of making these sorts of Jewish continuities explicit. His version of Jesus's gospel story always tries to bring the Hebrew scriptures to a close. That story is now fulfilled, he believes, and his gospel is intended to close the book at last.

If Luke's Jesus manages his escape through prayer, and Mark's Jesus—as we will see—is locked inside a tragedy he cannot escape, then Matthew's Jesus stands somehow in the middle. It almost appears as if there are two Jesuses in Matthew's version, only one of whom can be tragic. The pathos of Jesus's abandonment is as desperate as it was in Luke, but the ambiguity runs deeper. Two very different sorts of reasoning seem to be in place—one at Matthew 26:39–42, and another at Matthew 26:53–54—and they seem to work at cross purposes. Remember Matthew's main point: a human soul can be torn in two. Jesus is at one and the same time the man who begs God for deliverance ("My Father, if it is possible, . . ."; Matthew 26:39), but also the mighty prophet at whose command stand all the legions of heaven ("Do you suppose it is impossible . . ."; Matthew 26:53). He is a man who vaguely senses that it is impossible for him to escape death ("My Father, if it is not possible . . ."; Matthew 26:42), and yet he is also a great seer who clearly discerns the necessity of God's will ("But then how could the scriptures be fulfilled . . . ?"; Matthew 26:54). So Jesus is two things at once, and the way he prays illustrates this quite clearly. That duality in Jesus's character is something neither Mark nor John could really accept, and most later Christian battles would be waged under one of their two banners. Mark's Jesus is human, all too human; John's Jesus is divine. Mark's Jesus will give eloquent voice to all of his doubt and pain; John's Jesus never doubts a thing.

Mark's Story

Last of the three, his face half-hidden in shadows cast by the dwindling firelight, is a man named Mark, who, rumor has it, once knew Jesus's best friend Peter, followed him to Rome, and then managed to get out of town at the very last moment when Peter was killed there. The names get fuzzy here, of course, because Peter's name wasn't really Peter; that's just the Greek version of an Aramaic nickname that Jesus gave to the man whose real name was Simon. The nickname—*Cephas* in Aramaic and *Petros* in Greek—simply meant "Rock," and this nickname was believed to speak to his rock-hard steadiness of character. But if you know Mark's story (and keep in mind that Mark knew Peter personally and got his story from the man), then the nickname's a little ironic, unless by "rock" Jesus really meant "volcano." No matter; as Mark knows better than anyone, virtuous people can do vicious things. That is a large part of the tragedy of human life.

Marcus is a Roman name, but there's no telling where in the Roman Empire the man we know as Mark was from. Thus even by name, he's something of a mystery and utterly unique. He doesn't look like anyone else, he doesn't talk like anyone else, and he doesn't think like anyone else either. The way he keeps to himself, the way he can be so quiet for such lengths of time, makes guessing his mind even harder to do. So he lets them wait; Mark always makes them wait. And he doesn't mind going last, because in the topsy-turvy world he has come to believe is the only true one, the last will be first someday. He is living proof of that. When he speaks, his gravelly voice has a viselike grip that won't let the audience go. And his accent, though it sounds strange at first, grows on you like a habit, like a vine. It doesn't let you go. Here is how he starts. "I'll tell you the story if you really want to hear it. But you won't like it much, and if you do, then you haven't understood."

And they came to a region, whose name is Gethsemane, and Jesus said to his students, "Sit here while I pray." And he took Peter and James and John along with him, and he began to be agitated and greatly distressed, and he said to them, "My soul is in agony until death. Stay here and watch." And he went on a little farther and fell upon the ground, and he prayed that, if possible, the hour might pass him by; and he said, *"Abba, the Father, all things are possible for you. Take this cup away from me. Still, not what I want, but what you do."*

And he came and found them sleeping, and he said to Peter, "Simon, are you sleeping? Were you not strong enough to watch one hour? Watch and pray that you may not enter into

55

temptation. The spirit is willing, but flesh is weak." And again he went away and prayed, saying the same thing. And when he returned, again he found them sleeping, for their eyes were heavy, and they did not know how to respond to him. And when he came a third time he said to them, "You are still sleeping and resting? Get up. The hour has come. Behold, the Son of Man is betrayed into the hands of sinners. Get up; let's go. Behold, my betrayer draws near."

And immediately, while he was still speaking, Judas came, one of the Twelve, and with him a crowd armed with swords and clubs, along with the chief priests and the scribes and the elders. The betrayer had given them a common sign, saying, "The one I kiss will be the man. Seize him and lead him away under close guard." And going immediately to him, Judas said, "Rabbi," and he kissed him. Then they lay their hands upon him and seized him. Someone standing nearby drew his sword and struck the slave of the high priest and cut off his ear. And Jesus, responding, said to them, "Have you come out against me like a criminal, with swords and clubs? Every day I was with you in the temple teaching and you did not seize me. But the scriptures shall be fulfilled." And all left him alone and fled.

Now a young man followed behind him, with a robe cast over his naked body, and they seized him too. But leaving the robe behind, he also fled, naked [Mark 14:32–52].

The first will be last, Mark tells us (at Mark 9:35 and 10:43–45). We are finally in a position to confront his version of the Gethsemane story, to hear its raw power and tragic virtuosity anew. While Mark was the first of the Synoptic gospels to be written down, we are reading him last in order to see more clearly how different his version really is. And how bleak.

It was Mark who gave the place a name. Gethsemane comes from the Hebrew word for "oil presses," an appropriate name for a spot traditionally held to be located on or close to the Mount of Olives. Jesus immediately instructs his disciples to sit, while he goes off to pray. It is a strange thing to say, given that it is never clear how alone Mark's Jesus can ever really be. Mark's Jesus lives within a series of strange concentric circles: his favorite three disciples; then the twelve; then other disciples and fellow travelers; and finally, the swelling crowds who never leave him in peace. In the relative privacy of Gethsemane, Jesus takes his innermost circle—Peter, James, and John—with him, apart from all the others. This directly recalls the first parable Jesus tells in Mark's gospel (Mark 4:1–9). As an image of God's Kingdom and its mysterious workings, Jesus describes the scattering of a great quantity of seed, the vast majority of which fails to take root, withers, and dies. Mark's whole gospel can be read as the dramatic enactment of this parable.[13] As Jesus moves decisively south to Jerusalem, the crowd gradually falls away. By sundown on the evening of what we know will be his last, only twelve are left, and we know that one of them has the heart of a betrayer. Now, with Judas gone, other disciples are peeled away, and only three remain. Jesus leaves them behind as well and "goes on a little farther" (Mark 14:35) to pray. Everything is upside down. When Jesus wants to be alone, he can't be. When he wants and needs friends, they abandon him. And now, in prayer, the communion he seeks with his God ends with further and final

*Jesus is
alone* (handwritten margin note)

abandonment. Even in prayer, Mark's Jesus is alone. No answer comes to him, unless betrayal and arrest count as answers. It is all unbearably sad. Then God's messiah and Son, abandoned, agonized, and alone, is swallowed up into the crowd again, when it invades his privacy one final time and kills him.

Jesus's first parable about the scattering of seed offers an important interpretive clue for understanding what Mark is trying to show us in Gethsemane. Jesus concluded that parable with what becomes a haunting refrain in Mark's gospel: "He who has ears to hear, let him hear" (Mark 4:9). Translated this way, Jesus's words are not only paradoxical; they actually seem unfair. Those with ears *have to* hear, after all; they are passive recipients of the words God has sown. But if we translate this phrase afresh as "He who has ears to listen, let him listen," then the image changes. Now it is a question of taking action, of making the effort to listen to our surroundings. The difficulties of looking carefully, of listening well, and of understanding—the whole question of spiritual attention—are major preoccupations throughout Mark's gospel. Nothing comes easily in Mark's story—not to the disciples, and not to Jesus. And nothing at all is given for free. Mark is the purest nonfatalist at Gethsemane's quiet campfire; that is one hallmark of his tragic genius. For tragedy, as we will see, is not a pure act of fate; it is a contest of wills instead.

Mark's sudden use of the passive voice complicates the picture. Mark is interested not only in the inner world of his main characters but also in the fact that Jesus, here at the very end of his life, is more acted upon than actor. Jesus takes on an uncharacteristically passive role, in Gethsemane and from then on.

Whereas he has continually insisted that his disciples learn to act and think for themselves (Mark 6:7–13), now, in what is probably their first truly independent action, Judas acts decisively—and betrays the entire mission. Now Jesus, who has been the only one in full control of himself, finds himself in the control of a violent and violating world. Now Jesus "began to be agitated and greatly distressed" (Mark 14:33). "And now he said, 'My soul is in agony until death'" (Mark 14:34). Violently disturbed (Mark uses some intense and unusual Greek words in these descriptions) and radically alone, Mark's Jesus seeks his solace in God—solace that, as Mark emphasizes, he does not find. For Mark, not even prayer guarantees anything; his version is very far from Luke's telling. Jesus's prayer fully reflects this awful paradox: "Abba, the Father, all things are possible for you. Take this cup away from me. Still, not what I want, but what you do" (Mark 14:36).

The subtle details in Mark's way of praying should not be missed. Whereas Matthew and Luke both have Jesus address God personally (and whereas in John's version, the union between Jesus and God is virtually complete), here in Mark's gospel Jesus addresses a God who is suddenly and mysteriously very far away: "Abba, the Father."[14] In short, Jesus is trying to maintain intimacy with a God who is lost. He asks that "this cup" be taken away, a request we have seen in every Synoptic account of this prayer. But that is where the similarities end. We are finally in a position to compare the decisive qualification Jesus makes in each performance of the Gethsemane prayer. In so doing, we will see careful attention paid to Jesus's will, especially in Luke's gospel, as well as to possibility and its relationship to scriptural fate in Matthew's and Mark's. As I will attempt to show in the next chapter, without these two categories—of will and of fate—there can be no real tragedy, no Greek conception of human destiny.[15]

I have set Jesus's actual prayer in italics in each Synoptic version to make it easier to notice the subtle differences. In one sense, all four storytellers are rivals around the same Christian campfire. In Luke's version, Jesus prays, "Father, *if you will,* take this cup away from me. Still, let not my will be done, but yours." This conditional stands out dramatically from what Jesus prays in the other Synoptic performances. In Matthew's story, Jesus prays, "My Father, *if it is possible . . .*" and then again, "*if it is not possible . . .*" In Mark's story, the conditions are just as we have seen: "Abba, the Father, *all things are possible to you . . .*"

Given the way he sets up the prayer, Luke's conclusion seems clear enough: Jesus's Father did not want (or "will") to take this cup of suffering away. Now, at the risk of returning you to your first college course in philosophy, I want to present three short syllogisms that owe their origins to the Gethsemane prayer. The sequence would be something like this, in Luke's version:

1. "Father, *if you will,* take this cup away from me."
2. The cup is not taken away.
3. God did not wish to remove it.

Luke's conclusion in Gethsemane is that God's will is otherwise, and gradually through prayer, Jesus's will disappears.

For Matthew, the implication seems to be that this cup cannot be avoided:

1. "My Father, *if it is possible,* take this cup from me."
2. The cup is not taken away.
3. It is not possible for God to remove it.

Matthew tells us why this is not possible in the end. According to him, the answer has something to do with scriptural fate. The script of Jesus's passion-play was written a very long time ago: "It is necessary that the writings of the prophets be fulfilled," he tells us repeatedly. Mark, in contrast, leaves the thing in its starkest form, and the question he poses cannot really have an answer:[16]

1. "Abba, the Father, *all things are possible for you.* Take this cup away from me."
2. The cup is not taken away.
3. We can only wonder why.[17]

The shocking implications of this way of praying can scarcely be overstated. Most of Mark's gospel is designed to create shocks like this. The extraordinary communion that Jesus has enjoyed with God, though seldom explicitly mentioned by Mark, has been graphically apparent in word and deed. John tells us about it; Mark *showed* it. Jesus's Father, while a God of few words, has been a God of decisive deeds. Now, quite suddenly, his silence speaks louder than his words or deeds have ever done. If we are not expecting Matthew's twelve legions of angels, we could at least expect a word of comfort. In point of fact, expectations of this kind have been carefully cultivated in Mark's gospel. Just prior to his arrival in Jerusalem, Mark's Jesus spoke with uncharacteristic confidence about the power of prayer: "Have faith in God. Truly, I say to you that if someone were to say to this mountain, 'Be lifted up and cast into the sea!' and if he is not divided in his heart, but believes that what he says will come to pass, then he shall have it" (Mark 11:22–23). Faithful prayer was supposed to be a certainty. Now Mark hits us with a brand-new worry: perhaps Jesus is divided in his heart, or perhaps this naive belief in the automatic power of prayer is the greatest Christian temptation. All things are possible with God. Jesus asks that the cup be taken away. It is not taken away. Full stop.

Next come the parts of the story we recognize. Jesus returns to his disciples and finds them asleep. This is a strange word in Mark's vocabulary—Jairus's daughter was said to be asleep when in fact she had died (Mark 5:35–43). For some reason, Jesus speaks to Peter alone: "Simon, are you sleeping? Were you not strong enough to watch one hour? Watch and pray that you may not enter into temptation. The spirit is willing, but flesh is weak" (Mark 14:37–38). New issues come into focus with that remark. First, Jesus refers to Peter by his old name, Simon. He is no longer a "rock"; maybe he never was. A harsh note of failure and even rejection has crept into Jesus's inner circle. The repetition of the word *watch* carries an echo from all the earlier references to looking and listening, especially in Jesus's parables. Those who have ears must listen; those with eyes must look. This invitation is now intensified, commanded: "Watch." Jesus has been saying this over and over again, for fully two chapters by now (note especially his words of caution in Mark 13:33–36). The disciples are not listening, and now their eyes are closed.

It is surprising that Mark should introduce the notion of temptation only now. Mark's account of the events following Jesus's baptism lacks any explicit temptation narrative, a highly dramatic story that both Matthew (4:1–11) and Luke (4:1–13) tell at length. If he knows stories like that, Mark chooses not to tell them. In Mark's wilderness, Jesus was not threatened or tempted; he was ministered to by angels (as he always used to be, until now, whenever he found himself in "lonely places").[18] Alone now for the first time, Jesus *is* tempted. The flesh *is* weak, no matter how willing the spirit. This is no less true for one anointed by God. The tragic dimension to Mark's Passion narrative—the tale of Jesus's suffering from his arrival in Jerusalem to the moment of his death—was dramatically captured by a complex and brilliant modern French mystic named Simone Weil (1909–1943). Here is how she captured it in one of her most famous essays, written in the middle of the Second World War, just two years two before her death: "Human suffering is laid bare, and we see it in a being who is at once divine and human. The accounts of the Passion show that a divine spirit, incarnate, is changed by misfortune, trembles before suffering and death, feels itself, in the depths of its agony, to be cut off from man and God."[19] That is the heart of the human tragedy, Jesus's as well as ours, as Mark sees it.

Mark's Jesus goes back and forth, from prayer to his disciples, three times. He asks in near amazement how they can still be asleep. It is enough, and the time has come (Mark 14:41). Peter had been told to watch (Mark 14:37) for one hour. That hour is now at an end, and no one is watching. All are sleeping; soon they will flee. A powerless Jesus now asks his disciples to "get up." In happier times, he had healed the sick and raised the "sleeping" with an admonition like that; now he can only call them to the test—and to their inevitable failure.

Judas arrives "immediately," accompanied by a crowd. Mark describes this crowd in all of its imposing, violent reality (John intensifies that description, whereas Luke excises it entirely). Mark's crowd is armed with "swords and clubs" and is composed of "chief priests and scribes and elders" (an unholy trinity for Mark, who clearly does not think of himself as a scribe but rather as a tragedian). And now we get the flashback that explains it all (Mark 14:44). The betrayer has already arranged with the crowd to single Jesus out by kissing him. He approaches his teacher ("Rabbi!") and kisses him. The crowd seizes him. The spare phrasing here, clauses piled on top of clauses, words on top of words, sets the tone perfectly. If it is simply and purely awful, then why pretty it up with more words?

Something altogether remarkable happens at this point in Mark's telling. We have heard the story before, in Luke and Matthew, but never this way. One of Jesus's anonymous follow-ers strikes the slave of the high priest and cuts off his ear. Only Mark tells us this without any elaboration. Jesus does not heal the ear; he does not say a word. The reasons for this are not hard to find. Jesus has continually insisted, almost as a man-tra, that those with ears must listen (Mark 4:9). That is what

God asks of us, pure and simple. It would not be too much to call "looking and listening" the very essence of discipleship in Mark's gospel. In the violent assault at Gethsemane, listening itself has become impossible. It is not clear if God is listening. A human ear has been intentionally severed by Jesus's own disciples. If those with ears must listen, what are those who have been deprived of ears supposed to do? The failure of all Jesus's followers to understand their mission or to hear what he has said could not be more dramatically represented. And it is precisely now that Jesus is spirited away.

Mark's gospel emphasizes the totality of the failure. *All* forsook him. *Everyone* fled. And yet—here is another story that only Mark will tell us—a mysterious and anonymous "young man" followed Jesus as the other disciples were unable to do, with only a linen cloth to cover his naked body.[20] When the crowd attempts to seize him, just as they seized Jesus, he drops his robe and flees. We might recall how important following was to Luke. The two verbs that refer to this anonymous young man tell us all we need to know about him: he *follows* and then he *flees*. Like everyone else in Mark's story, in the most fateful moment, he cannot stand where he intended to stand. Many scholars believe that Mark invites his readers to see him in the role of the Roman centurion who watched Jesus die and who recognized him in that moment as God's Son (Mark 15:39). That seems too optimistic for Mark's way of telling things. I think that Mark clearly identifies himself with this young man, and he insists that we should, too. Peter presumably told Mark how he failed Jesus this night. Now we are told that Mark failed him too—and yet he is still trying to tell the story. There is no other way to avoid religious triumphalism and hypocrisy than to focus on such relentlessly tragic truths.

Mark, as I hope it is clearer by now, has a remarkably dramatic touch. Christopher Burdon puts it this way, referring to the modern shift away from studying the gospels "historically":

> In the nineteenth century critics decided that Mark's was the first of the four Gospels to be written, and it was given much greater attention in the hope that it would yield really secure historical information about Jesus and his teaching. These hopes were not fulfilled. But it may be no accident that Mark has received serious attention *as a writer* only in the age of cinema. For he begins and ends his book abruptly; he gives us sudden changes of scene; he has flashbacks, stories inserted within stories ... that fast pace with all its *and*'s and *immediately*'s.[21]

Taking that image to heart—Mark the filmmaker and tragic storyteller—imagine where Mark's fireside story has left us. As the lights fade from the torches of the receding crowd and the curtain draws down over this scene, neither Jesus nor his disciples are visible. He has been swallowed up; they have all abandoned him. The last anonymous companion who attempted to follow in Jesus's way also fails. He fled too. The camera focuses, then slowly fades, on an abandoned linen robe, soiled and imperfectly folded, trampled by the crowd.[22]

John's Great Denial

There is a young man in this audience, his face nearly as hidden as Mark's was, but for different reasons—he actually believes there's a light in his own face that is so bright he needs to hide it, for now. By the time the evening's stories are done, he knows what he wants to be, knows what he wants to do with his life. He wants to tell the story of Jesus better than anyone else has ever told it. He wants it to be more shocking, more grandiose, spiced with more drama and absolutely no doubt. What he really wants is to steal the laurel wreath from this upstart mystery-man to whom even Matthew and Luke defer—there's something about Mark's frankness that is shocking, and the shock scares John, even at a distance. To do all this and capture his crown, he'll have to figure out a way to make himself even more "beloved" than Peter was—and Matthew and Luke and Mary and all the rest. The amazing thing is that he was destined to succeed, probably beyond his own wildly ambitious dreams. But to succeed, he had to change the story into something very different from the story Mark first told, the "gospel" that Matthew and Luke amplified and prettied up. And still more: the only way to sell this story, as John discovers much to his own dismay, is to take to the road and to tell it in other places, places where no one has heard Mark's story yet.

And thus, I suppose, is a new religion always born.

> When Jesus said these things, he went out with his students
> across the Kedron Valley where there was a garden; then he
> and his students entered it. Now Judas, the one who betrayed

him, also knew the place, since Jesus often gathered there with his students. So Judas took a body of soldiers from among the chief priests and Pharisees, and they went there with torches and lanterns and weapons.

Since Jesus already knew everything that was to happen to him, he went out and said to them, "Whom are you seeking?" And they answered him, "Jesus the Nazarene." He said to them, "I am." Judas, the one who betrayed him, was also standing among them. But when he said to them, "I am," they all fell back and fell upon the ground. Therefore, he asked them again, "Whom are you seeking?" And they said, "Jesus the Nazarene." Jesus responded, "I told you I am. If then you are looking for me, let these others go." This was in order to fulfill what the *logos*[23] said: "I lost none of all those you have given me."

Now Simon Peter had a sword and he drew it and struck the high priest's slave and cut off his right ear. The slave's name was Malchus. Then Jesus said to Peter, "Put the sword in its sheath. *The cup that the Father has given me—shall I not drink it?*" [John 18:1–11].

Clearly, the story of Jesus's prayer in Gethsemane was told very differently by the three Synoptic evangelists. There are trace fingerprints all over these stories, and everything hinges on the details—what Jesus specifically does and says, as well as what he hopes and what he fears. It is somewhat difficult to generalize about Gethsemane, to say in any simple way what it was supposed to be a story about. But this much we can say with some confidence: the Synoptic story of Gethsemane has three essential components: an ambiguous temptation, a prayer about a cup, and Judas's betrayal. Without these components, it would not be the story of Gethsemane, at least not as Mark and Matthew and Luke understood it. Many later gospels discovered at Nag Hammadi and elsewhere changed this story around. According to the gospel of Peter,[24] Jesus was not tempted at all; he actually laughed, all the way to the cross. According to the recently published gospel of Judas,[25] Jesus was not betrayed either. Rather, he insisted that his closest disciple—Judas, not Peter—do what he did in order to show us the way to escape from the world by "sacrificing the man that clothes me."[26] In this gospel, too, Jesus laughs a great deal. In their own ways, then, these so-called Gnostic gospels are as anti-tragic as John's evangel is. But these gospels were later deemed heretical. Ironically enough, John led the way in this heretical reconceiving of the gospel at Gethsemane. He was the first one to turn the story of Gethsemane on its head. The later Gnostic denials of Gethsemane are not so very different from John's. But somehow John crept into the canon. It is the questionable "orthodoxy" of John's account that is my primary concern in this book.

As I've pointed out, in John's evangel, the story of Gethsemane lacks two of its three essential components. There is no temptation, and there is no prayer. John, in fact, never shows us any explicit temptations of Jesus. This should seem less surprising by now. It would make little sense for a God-like Jesus ever to suffer temptation or fear; he is never alone, "for the Father is with [him] always" (John 16:31–32). And if John's Jesus suffers no human frailties or limitations, then it would make little sense for him to pray either. As indeed he does not.

69

What John's Jesus does instead is to refer disparagingly to the Gethsemane prayer—twice—as something the disciples, not Jesus, are tempted to say. Synoptic words are invoked by John, but to make the opposite point and all in a manner of mockery. Mark's tragedy is in real danger of transformation into a Christian farce. John's Jesus says, in utter self-transparency and complete self-control, "Now is my soul troubled. And what shall I say? 'Father, save me from this hour'? No, for this purpose I have come to this hour" (John 12:27). The tension that is to varying degrees internalized in the Synoptic accounts of Jesus's prayer in the face of a temptation is now externalized, made visible for all to see. It has become a fairly simple Christological monologue, intended to show how different Jesus is from the rest of us. The spirit is willing and the flesh (if Jesus really has flesh) is *strong*.

This is the moment when Mark's tragedy was turned inside out by a rival Christian, and his gospel was turned upside down. What happens in John's evangel is very simple: Jesus resolves to go south to Jerusalem for the last time; he refuses to pray for deliverance (John 12:27). John's Jesus does not *need* to pray; he has always been with the Father, and he is always resolute. What follows next, in place of Mark's poignant parables and Passion, are three rousing chapters of "I am" sayings (John 14–17), some of the most memorable lines in John's evangel.[27] Then and only then do we come to Gethsemane, which only John refers to as a "garden." What happens here will be—in contrast to all three Synoptic gospels—just another triumph. The mention of a garden can't help but call Eden to mind.[28] And for John, this garden is the place where God

Himself will finally undo the damage done by his disobedient creatures in the first one. There is no scandal, no turmoil, no tragedy, only triumph.

Beyond some similarities in surface details, cobbled together from the other evangelists, John's virtuoso performance of the Gethsemane story is unique. John tells us that Jesus "already knew everything that was to happen to him" (John 18:4), and so he takes command even in the situation where he is to be betrayed and arrested. *The lamb is leading the priests to his own sacrifice.* Jesus boldly approaches the heavily armed crowd (John 18:3) and literally imposes himself on them: "Whom are you seeking?" (John 18:4). When the crowd learns that he is the man they seek, strangely enough, they fall away in fear and then fall to the ground. So Jesus forces the issue a second time, actually forces the crowd to seize him, in order, he suggests, that what the *Logos* has said may be fulfilled. This is a detail and a mode of reasoning that John has borrowed from Matthew, but as always, he changes what he borrows, turning it to his own purposes (John 18:9). John is not interested in showing how Jesus's life fulfilled Jewish prophecies, because he has given up on the Jews and on Judaism. He is more interested in proving that Jesus is God's incarnate *Logos.*

John fights on many fronts at once. He is attempting to replace Matthew's and Luke's gospels, and he is working heroically to turn Mark's gospel upside down. John is out to supplant Peter's authority, Thomas's authority, Mary's authority, and that of all the other disciples. John is fundamentally opposed to pagan Greeks, and he has declared war on Judaism and the Jews. Judas is the clearest symbolic marker of this last aspect of John's evangel. Whereas the Synoptic performances all define him primarily by his activity (he is simply "the betrayer"), John underlines his name. That name, Judas (*Ioudas*), sounds virtually identical to the Greek word for "Jew" (*Ioudaios*). Now, we cannot know how Greek names were regarded in antiquity by John's audience, any more than we can determine how many people today think of cabinetmaking when introduced to a person named Carpenter. But what does seem clear is that John very carefully links the Jews to this act of divine betrayal, betrayal being virtually the only aspect of Mark's story that John has kept. This is a prominent feature in John's evangel, which goes to extraordinary lengths to intensify its polemic against a Jewish community that has seen Jesus but refused to believe in him[29] and that had recently kicked Christians out of its synagogues (a virtual transcript of how that happened may be found in chapter 9 of John's evangel, as we will see).

In fact, John's garden scene may be neatly divided in two parts, each containing the same phrase: "Judas, the one who betrayed him." At the beginning, in the garden, we are told that "Judas, the one who betrayed him, knew the place" (John 18:2). The second half of the story is introduced in the same way: "and Judas, the one who betrayed him, was standing among them" (John 18:5). I have noticed a lot of doubled tellings in these performances, most dramatically in Matthew's version of Jesus's prayer. Here, in John, both halves contain the same repeated exchanges, exchanges that confirm Jesus's divine control of the situation, his astounding otherworldliness and nonhumanity. In other words, John's Jesus may say things twice, but the doubling changes nothing.

Whom do you seek? (v. 4)	Whom do you seek? (v. 7)
Jesus the Nazarene. (v. 5)	Jesus the Nazarene. (v. 7)
I am. (v. 5)	I told you I am. (v. 8)

When Matthew repeated Jesus's prayer a second time, the words were subtly different. Jesus's mind is divided and changing. In John, as I say, repetition changes nothing. John's Jesus is a figure of astonishing resolve, timeless and immovable. Unlike Luke's Jesus, he does not need to pray to gain resolve or self-control. He and his father are one, so he never needs to pray. Gethsemane is in fact a drama that he has anticipated since the beginning of time. It is only the crowd that wavers, when it first moves to seize him. After the first exchange, the crowd falls away from him, presumably in awe of his courage (when he tells them "I am") and his mystical otherness (when his answer invokes God's name: "I am"). It is only Jesus's persistence that ensures that this will be done. Jesus, the shepherd of his people and perhaps also the divine author of this script, draws the conclusion for a crowd that seems unwilling to go there unless it is led. John's irony runs deep; they are not captors but sheep. And Jesus is the new high priest who will make himself both lamb and shepherd at once. The scene concludes with the shepherd's steadfast concern for his sheep: "If then you are looking for me, let these others go" (John 18:8).

Next, Simon Peter draws a sword and cuts off the right ear of a slave named Malchus (John 18:10).[30] It is curious that both of these characters—Peter and Malchus—are named only by John. Names are very much on John's mind—how they sound and what they mean. But here, it is as if John wants to assure us that he was there, that he saw it all himself. As we will see repeatedly, John is constantly working to establish his own authority and to supplant that of the others, especially the Synoptic gospel writers.

The Synoptic story of Gethsemane raised two critical questions that are nearly impossible to answer. First, if Jesus was alone when he prayed, then how can anyone know exactly what he said? Second, if Jesus was on such intimate terms with God, then how can their wills be so dramatically out of sync at the very end of the story? John's evangel cuts the complicated Gordian knot of such questions with a very simple answer: Jesus didn't pray that way. Everything is very public and very straightforward in John's evangel; the people are just too sheepish or too stupid to accept what they are told and what they see. John's Jesus does not pray in private. In fact, the scene concludes with Jesus's repeated *mockery* of the Gethsemane prayer: "The cup that the Father has given me—shall I not drink it?" (John 18:11).

If the Synoptic story of Gethsemane is a story about praying in the face of temptation prior to betrayal, then John's is no longer the same story at all. As I pointed out earlier, of the three elements that seem indispensable to the tragic story of Gethsemane, John retains only the betrayal—and even that is handled differently. The very phrases that lent such pathos and humanity to the Synoptic Passion narrative—"Father, . . . take this cup away from me"—are uttered now by a Jesus whose voice is dripping with irony. These are presumably sentiments for lesser mortals, not the *Logos* of God. And this is how the essence of the tragedy lying at the heart of the Gethsemane story has been undone. Though John borrows freely from the other gospels, he changes what he takes to suit his own purposes, and he does so always with an eye to *replacing* them. He thus ends up telling a very different story in a very different way. Jesus, the incarnate champion of the divine will, seizes the cup that has been given him, and drinks it to the dregs. Nothing less, it seems, could be expected of the mysterious being who "has conquered the world" (John 16:33).

Personal Marks

What I have tried to do in this chapter, true to my archaeological predilections, is to pick up the gospels, one at a time, and to examine them more closely for their authors' fingerprints. The personal mark of each author is clearly visible in Gethsemane. At a minimum, we can discern what the gospel writers were against by noticing the way they tell us who they think Jesus was and what he stood for. In Mark's case, it is very clear: Mark's Jesus was against religious hypocrisy and all forms of religious triumphalism that so often travel clothed with religious pride. He worried especially about triumphalist Christian rhetoric that suggested that God's gospel had somehow conquered pain and death. It is clear from the way Mark tells Jesus's story that many Christians were already talking in this way, pridefully marching toward martyrdom as if it were a Roman triumph. Like Luke, they were telling a story they think we'd like to hear. Mark does not. He tells us that Jesus was really a man, really embodied, and that he really died in horrible pain and mental anguish on a Roman cross. Then he stops right there, forcing us to think more about that. The account is shattering in its starkness and simplicity.

In short, Jesus's story was a tragedy as Mark understood it, and it remained at least loosely tragic in the other two Synoptic gospels. But John's story—what I have been calling his evangel—is a shocking *denial* of Christian tragedy. If Mark modeled his gospel on Greek tragedy, then John has given us the first of many subsequent divine comedies. But in so doing, John had to erase the dramatic episode that Mark located in Gethsemane—a powerful story about prayer and temptation, about the sheer humanity of Jesus's doubts and the awful depth of his suffering. Mark's tragedy hinges on the fact that we are witnesses to the collision between two wills, a tragic struggle for self-definition in which we are invited to participate and to recognize as our own. John simply cannot tell a story like that because his theology cannot allow for a collision of wills between Father and Son or for a divided picture of Jesus. John's Jesus is so heroically self-present, so transparent to the divine will, that he cannot experience tragedy or hopeless suffering. John's Jesus cannot pray for deliverance either, since Jesus's execution is presented as yet another triumph, not a scandal. We are as close to the heresy of crude triumphalism and Christian death wish as we will ever be in the New Testament. Christians even at the time noticed this, and many of them wondered how John's evangel could be compatible with the Synoptic gospels at all. Some wondered if John's evangel should even be on the list of acceptable Christian readings.

Some wondered if it was heretical. Some wondered how such an anti-tragic story could be Christian—or true.

Mark's gospel might best be seen as a dramatic illustration of the true nature of being schooled in the tragic way of Jesus. It is a story about the difficulty of discipleship as much as it is about Jesus. In short, it is written *for us*. No cheap optimism disrupts the tragic tones in which Mark paints such schooling. "I believe . . . but help my unbelief" (Mark 9:24) is about the best that a human being can ever say.[31] Souls are divided; that never changes. Mark's is a tragedy that leads *necessarily* from Gethsemane, to abandonment, to the cross. To find your life, you must lose it first. There is also a terrifying identity between Jesus and his disciples in Mark's gospel. Jesus's road will be their road, completely—even if they do not understand this yet (Mark 10:38). And that is the tragic heart of Mark's gospel.

CHAPTER THREE

Mark's Tragic Gospel

The Birth of a Christian Genre

I think it may be taken as established that drama—all drama—grew from a sacrificial contest ending in a death and some sort of transfiguration. Agony is the heartbeat; death is the crucible; renewal is the goal. These are the terms by which drama may be identified. They are all serious terms, and death stands at their center inflexible and indispensable, the key, the passport, the *sine qua non*. . . . Tragedy must stand in the way. It *is* the way.

—WALTER KERR, *TRAGEDY AND COMEDY* (1967)

Greek tragedy begins where Munch's *Scream* leaves off—staring dumbly into atrocity. . . . After atrocity, poetry is the only adequate response. . . . In the theater I most admire, poets, and I stress poets, wrote for actors they knew and for a space they knew.

—TONY HARRISON, QUOTED IN *ARION* (2007)

If Luke was half poet and half historian, if Matthew was a Jewish disciple who believed Jesus had fulfilled the scriptures, and if John was the highly ambitious evangelist who intended to take their place by claiming to be most beloved by Jesus, then what was Mark? The short answer, which I have been suggesting all along and will develop further in this chapter, is that Mark was a tragedian, a Christian poet building on the classical Greek models of Aeschylus, Sophocles, Euripides, and their countless Roman imitators. The shock of such a claim is twofold for a modern Christian audience. First, tragedy is commonly thought to be Christianity's troubling opposite, a genre that focuses on bad news, not the "good news" of the Christian gospel. Moreover, tragedy is a pagan Greek genre, whose countless gods and goddesses and their endless misbehavior are believed to have nothing to do with the sober God of Abraham and Moses and his unforgiving Law. I want to address both of these areas of confusion before turning to the substance of Mark's remarkable literary achievement.

First, on the Greekness of Greek tragedy. The existence of so many tragedies from the classical Greek world (some thirty-three plays in total, with fragments of many more) suggests that for the Christian monks who lovingly copied them over and passed them on to future generations, there was no necessary incompatibility between Greek tragedies and the new way they believed had been inscribed in their gospels. We even have one late antique document, the *Christus Patiens,*[1] which actually cobbles together a Christian tragedy almost entirely out of lines and couplets borrowed from Greek dramas that its author clearly studied in school[2] and used as literary models. So some later Christian poets and theologians clearly believed that they could use Greek tragedy to make Christian meaning. That is the stunning creative achievement that I am suggesting Mark first imagined. His conceptual genius has only now begun to receive the recognition it deserves.

Tragedy and Philosophy

Perhaps the most remarkable thing to note at the outset is that the entire New Testament, including all four gospels, was written in Greek, not Aramaic.[3] Language and translation were never minor matters to ancient people; the decision by some Jews in Alexandria in the third century B.C.E. to translate the Hebrew scriptures into Greek was recognized to be the frank admission of a fairly radical change in the very fabric of their society and its beliefs. Some Jews worried whether this translation into Greek would inevitably alter the truth of their ancient Hebrew revelation. And in a real way, the new world created by the conquests of Alexander the Great (who died in 323 B.C.E.) and the encounters of many peoples—from Anatolia, Persia, India, and Egypt—with Greek culture created the crucible in which rabbinic Judaism, Christianity, and Gnosticism all emerged. The eastern Mediterranean was a Greek world, and its very Greekness opened a door onto a new world of spiritual possibilities, possibilities the Synoptic gospels were designed to examine in detail. Thus the New Testament is an important chapter in the history of Greek literature.

That said, for me to suggest that the essence of that literature was "tragic" may still raise concerns, if not actual Christian hackles. Didn't Dante recognize the Christian message as a divine *comedy,* not a tragedy? Naturally, that depends on what you mean by comedy, what you mean by tragedy, and how you understand the relationship between the two. As the great Broadway theater critic Walter Kerr explained with stunning eloquence, if you wish to write about comedy, then you must write about tragedy too. (Plato said much the same thing.)[4] When he first tried to write a book about comedy, Kerr admits, in initial shock and then dawning comprehension, "tragedy kept getting in the way."[5] It took him a bit longer to realize that tragedy *is* the way.

We possess some important new resources for imagining Greek tragedy, in its own context and in ours.[6] Greek tragedies began to fascinate Europeans and North Americans all over again in the nineteenth century. Romantic poets translated them; famous actors performed them; modern dancers choreographed them; New Age adepts tried to use them for spiritual enlightenment. And the whole corpus of Greek tragedy, as well as philosophical meditations on Greek tragedy, beginning with Aristotle's *Poetics*—all of which had been central texts in the Italian Renaissance—washed over the intellectual landscape of modern Europe (and then, a century later, of North America as well). The first modern philosopher who wrestled explicitly with tragedy was Georg Wilhelm Friedrich Hegel (1770–1831). What is most remarkable about Hegel's tragic musings is how little they have been appreciated.[7] Indeed, most of the criticisms made of Hegel's philosophy—that it is too optimistic, that it doesn't take human suffering seriously enough, that it tries to make everything work out in the end—specifically contradict everything Hegel said about what made Greek tragedy so enduring and so important.[8]

For Hegel, tragedy was fundamentally about what he called "collision," specifically, the inevitable moral collisions that pervade the lives of human beings. Collisions occur, he noted, because there is more than one will in the world.

Though we may be conflicted within ourselves, undecided or "of two minds," we can never really collide with ourselves in the way that we may collide with other people, whose minds are not our own. That shattering moment of collision—and the opportunity for transformation that such collision makes possible—requires the existence of another person, another will. For Hegel, all selves are social selves, even God's, and society is the ethical realm that emerges out of the collisions between such selves and in what flows between them in such elevated and difficult moments of encounter. To explain what he had in mind, Hegel distinguished between what he called "horizontal" and "vertical" Greek tragedies. Like Aristotle, Hegel was especially fond of Sophocles, and like Aristotle, he considered Sophocles's *Oedipus the King* one of the greatest of all ancient dramas (admittedly, as a modern person, Hegel was also able to discuss Shakespeare and Christianity, as Aristotle could not—I'll return to that point in a moment).

Hegel used Sophocles's *Antigone* as an exemplary model for horizontal tragedy. In that play, we see the necessary collision between two forms of ethical duty. The first is the sister's duty to bury her dead brother, the fundamental point where honor, grief, and loss meet; it is also arguably the moral moment out of which all human society emerges. (This, by the way, is why the women's trip to the tomb to attend to Jesus's body is a matter of such enormous ethical significance. It is interesting that the conducting of such rites for the dead seems to be the special work of women in ancient societies.) The other ethical duty is the preservation of order in a city torn apart by civil war, a city now very near the breaking point and descent into anarchy. Oedipus's son, Polyneices, attacks the city of Thebes to seize the throne from his brother, Eteocles. The two meet in battle outside the city gates and kill each other there. In the king's absence, the provisional ruler, Creon, decrees that Eteocles will receive burial with full honors, whereas the other brother, the usurper, will be left on the field uncovered, to be mutilated by animals. Their sister, Antigone, disobeys the decree, and buries her brother in the name of what she calls "the unwritten laws of the gods"; she is sentenced to death for doing so. This play is partly about civil disobedience and partly about religious belief and its relation to ethical action, but it is all about the collision between the two titanic wills of Antigone and Creon. And the end result of this play, for Hegel, is a new conception of ethics and politics and selfhood, and their not-so-simple relationship to one another.

Hegel's exemplary model of a vertical tragedy was Sophocles's *Oedipus the King* (a play that impressed Sigmund Freud a century later). Here the conflict of wills is more vertical than longitudinal, not so much a conflict between the will of the legislature or the king and a disobedient citizen, but rather between the will of the hero and the will of the gods. Oedipus receives an oracle suggesting that he is fated to kill his father and marry his mother. What is telling, for Hegel, is what happens next. Oedipus rebels against his fate; he actually believes that he can escape it. He literally tries to outrun his fate, by leaving town and abandoning the couple he believes to be his parents, so that he will never do what the oracle has predicted that he will do. The great paradox, and the great artistry, of Sophocles's play is the way it demonstrates that

Oedipus's desire to escape his fate is the very thing that brings it about. Oedipus kills an older man on the road leading away from Delphi; later, when he arrives in the city of Thebes, he finds the city in mourning over the loss of its king, and he takes the place of that king by marrying the queen. Eventually, and inevitably much too late, Oedipus discovers his crime. He was abandoned in infancy, rescued by a shepherd, and raised by a couple he mistakenly took to be his parents; it is this royal family, the king and queen of Thebes, who were his real parents— and he has in fact killed the king, his father, and married the queen, his mother. In a rage of grief, initial disbelief, and final fury, Oedipus blinds himself so as not to see the evidence of his crimes: the faces of his incest-bred children (these are the very children who will later play out their own tragedies before the walls of Thebes. Nearly all of them die there). Here the will of Oedipus to avoid his crimes collides with the will of the gods, expressed first in an oracle and later in fact. Paradoxically, this collision is the very thing that brings those crimes about, and yet along with the crimes, Oedipus gains a new depth of self-understanding. Oedipus will eventually become a god himself, as we learn when Sophocles returns to these themes in the very last play he wrote, *Oedipus at Colonus*.

The novelty of Hegel's philosophical analysis of tragedy lay in his suggestion that, according to these very categories, the Synoptic gospels were indeed Christian tragedies. The genius of Mark's gospel particularly lay in the way it combines the themes of horizontal and vertical tragedy in a single story. Jesus's collisions with the religious and political authorities of his day is exacerbated by the collisions between his will and

God the Father's. That collision detonates Mark's whole gospel, and the heart of that collision is the Gethsemane prayer. I hope it is clearer now why I focused so intently on the form of that prayer and why I am making so much of it. Mark made much of it.

Several important things followed, for Hegel, based on what he understood about Greek tragedy. First and foremost, the categories of "optimism" and "pessimism" simply make no sense when one speaks of tragedy. When modern people suggest that comedies are optimistic and tragedies are pessimistic, they are missing the whole point of tragedy, and they miss the intimate connection between the two. The source of our confusion, for Hegel, lay in the modern obsession with endings, with focusing on how things turn out in the end. Using Shakespeare's plays as models, modern theatergoers wrongly suggest that tragedies end badly and comedies end well. In Shakespeare's case, tragedies are thought to end with multiple murders (like the bloodbath at the end of *Hamlet*), whereas comedies end with one marriage or more (think of the end of *A Midsummer Night's Dream*). That was not true of Greek tragedy, Hegel insisted (and it doesn't even work for Shakespeare, which is why scholars refer to so many of his later dramas as "problem plays"). Hegel is clearly right about that. Roughly one-half of all the Greek tragedies we still possess end well, which is to say that one of their chief conflicts and collisions is resolved. But Greek tragedy never lets us forget the enormous price paid to achieve this resolution. Tragedy is neither optimistic nor pessimistic; it is realistic. It emphasizes what the gospels emphasize as well: that the path to glory (*doxa*) must pass through suffering (*pathos*). Aeschylus said much the same thing about *pathos,* with his repeated choral refrains designed to remind us that "suffering teaches." Edith Hamilton's luminous translation of one of Aeschylus's most famous choral odes from the *Agamemnon* renders this beautifully, I think:

> God, whose law it is
> that he who learns must suffer.
> And even in our sleep
> pain that cannot forget
> falls drop by drop
> upon the heart
> and in our own despite,
> against our will,
> comes wisdom to us
> by the awful grace God.[9]

Hegel rendered this insight even more pithily in a letter to a friend that I quoted in the Introduction: "Salvation is *through* suffering, not *from* it."[10] I am suggesting that it was Mark who said this first, in a combined Greek and Christian idiom, and in a genre he invented: the gospel.

What this suggests is surprising, even stunning, in its implications. Tragedy is actually about *redemption,* the only kind of redemption that is available, the only kind worth having, the *tragic* kind. Friedrich Nietzsche (1844–1900), who was a blinding critic of syrupy forms of Christian optimism, was not a blind critic of Jesus (I agree with Albert Schweitzer that Christians *should* read Nietzsche and should heed his repeated warnings about the perversion of Christian compassion in modern times). Moreover, Nietzsche was yet another nineteenth-century German philosopher (in reality, he was a classics professor) who got his start and found his bearings by reading ancient Greek tragedy. He has been as badly misunderstood as Hegel has been.[11] Nietzsche actually had great sympathy with a version of the gospel like Mark's; he had no time for the false promises and anti-tragic posturing of John.

Perhaps the most stunning image in all of Nietzsche's many reflections on Greek tragedy came in his very first book, *The Birth of Tragedy out of the Spirit of Music,* originally published in 1872 (a decade later, he changed the subtitle of the book to *Hellenism and Pessimism* to make his point about endings clearer). In this book, Nietzsche began with the observation of a fundamental psychological and physiological irony: pain and pleasure are often linked; laughter and crying begin in the same place in the human diaphragm. Nietzsche expanded on this idea with a lovely poetic image: if you stare at the sun for some time, you will begin to see dark spots before your eyes. The Greeks, Nietzsche suggests, stared so long into the darkness that they eventually began to see spots of light.[12] They turned that light into music. And that alchemical moment, he insists, was the miraculous moment when tragedy was born.

Mark knew this and more. What I am suggesting is that in the version of the gospel Mark created, Jesus stared into that same darkness, in a place called Gethsemane. His will collided with God's will there. He did not run, and he did not turn away from this hard truth, and eventually he caught a glimpse of brilliant, if terrifying, light. The music that Mark made of that moment is what we still call a gospel today.

Tragedy and Gospel

Now, one obvious objection to what I have just described will already have occurred to many readers. Mark never read Hegel or Nietzsche, so what possible insight can come from our reading those authors to understand Mark's gospel? It is an important question, but it has a clear answer, and that answer is important to understanding what I am trying to clarify in this book. Mark never read Hegel or Nietzsche; that is true. But Hegel and Nietzsche both read and appreciated Mark, and they both read him against the grain, as it were, by reading him alongside of Greek tragedy. The really dramatic assumption that has significantly advanced our understanding of the gospels is the suggestion that many recent New Testament scholars—including George Kennedy, Dennis MacDonald, and Vernon Robbins—have made about how Greek the Synoptic gospels are in conception and design. Mark, they suggest, has this in common with Hegel and Nietzsche: Mark knew Homer and Greek tragedy, and he modeled his new genre on theirs. The implications of that crucial Christian innovation are enormous. Mark's gospel carries the exciting possibility of reimagining Christianity as a tragic faith, one in which the virtue of a certain kind of compassion is its most distinguishing characteristic. "Pity and fear" are the fundamental emotions tragedy is designed to create, according to Aristotle;[13] Mark combined them with great artistry, thereby adding compassion to the tragic mix.

Aristotle also emphasized what he called the "wholeness" of a tragic drama. Tragedies could and should be staged at one sitting.[14] Aristotle emphasized this, but he did *not* say, as his Renaissance translators believed he had said, that a tragedy's dramatic action should be presented as if it happened all in a single day. Aristotle explained his conception of "wholeness" by suggesting that a tragedy needs to have a clear beginning, middle, and end.[15] Mark clearly understood the importance of this idea, conceptually as well as dramatically, and he built these categories into his gospel as well. In a world where most Christians hear the gospel only a few verses at a time, the raw power of Mark's gospel performance as a whole is easily lost.

In Greek, the first word of Mark's gospel is in fact *beginning*. He presents his work as "the *beginning* of the *gospel* of Jesus, the messiah (*christos*), the Son of God."[16] That last, somewhat strange designation, so Greek-sounding and so difficult for us to comprehend—the *Son* of God—is a complex title that comes up decisively three times in Mark's gospel: at the beginning, in the middle, and at the end. When Jesus is baptized by John in the Jordan River (Mark 1:9), he receives a vision when he comes up out of the water. A dove descends from the heavens and speaks to him alone: "You are my beloved Son; in you I am well pleased" (Mark 1:11). In the middle of Jesus's travels, and at the very midpoint of Mark's gospel, the same title recurs. Jesus has ascended a mountain with Peter and James and John, and he is suddenly transformed into a quasi-celestial being whom they see conversing with Moses and Elijah. Once again a voice comes from the heavens, speaking to all three of them this time: "This is my beloved Son; listen to him" (Mark 9:7). As in the beginning, as in the middle, so too at the end. When Jesus finally dies on the cross, in an agony of pain and desolation and despair, a Roman centurion somehow comes to an understanding of what his suffering has meant: "Truly, this man was the Son of God" (Mark 15:39), he says, in shocked and belated recognition. This is a crucial point for Mark's tragic gospel: the man is convinced by seeing Jesus die, not by seeing him raised up. So the cumulative impact of Mark's beginning, middle, and end is to establish that Jesus was the Son of God. But what can this possibly mean? And what can it mean that the "Son of God" was killed so tragically?

Mark's gospel is surprisingly short on simple answers. All we can say with confidence is that Mark's Jesus is dynamite. He erupts onto the scene as an adult—no cute little stories from childhood for this gospel writer; he is writing a tragedy, not a comedy of manners. And he erupts onto a very tense political scene in Roman Palestine. He is baptized by John, then immediately spirited away to the desert, where he is "tempted" by Satan (scholars such as Susan Garrett have devoted tremendous energy and creativity to thinking about what that means because it is not clear, and Mark says no more about it;[17] the issue comes up again in Gethsemane). John is arrested; Jesus takes over his mission. He immediately calls a circle of disciples to himself (Mark 1:16–20), mostly pairs of brothers, many of whom he gives new nicknames. But Jesus is a mystery to everyone, even to those who would seem to know him best. They know him and yet they don't; the point of a tragedy is not necessarily understanding it right away, and the point of dynamite is the detonation. There is only one thing everyone agrees about: Jesus speaks with authority (Mark 1:22). Jesus clearly detonated something in the tinderbox of Galilee, but very few have understood what it was, in Mark's judgment. It is far easier to deal with Jesus's troubling message by turning it into something it was not intended to be, something easier to understand and easier to bear. But to do that is a profound failure of tragic wisdom, in Mark's eyes. It fails to be true to Jesus; it is equally untrue to his message of divine compassion.

Mark's Jesus does not obey the law, *any* law, whether Jewish or Roman. He is almost scandalously dismissive of both. Laws are for people, not the other way around. That is the heart of the horizontal collisions in this gospel. Jesus teaches in parables to confuse people, not to help them (that is the astonishing message of chapter 4). He engages in some very strange and very public healings and then orders people not to tell anyone about them. Unsurprisingly, when he casts a whole host of demons into a herd of swine and they drown themselves in the sea, people *do* talk about it; the word spreads like wildfire (that is the shocking image in chapter 5, and from that point on, Jesus will never be able to escape the press of the crowds again). Next, John the Baptist is beheaded by a local puppet king who was placed on the throne by the Romans (Mark 6:14–29). Jesus understands what is happening; if Herod could do that to John, then he can and will do worse to Jesus. So Jesus begins to emphasize the tragic heart of his message: the only path to glory or redemption is through suffering. This is the one and only thing he says plainly (Mark 8:32). His followers do not want to hear it; most all of them do not.

Things come to a head, right in the middle, in chapter 8. Jesus asks his disciples who people think that he is. There are many speculations about that, as we might imagine. He is a great prophet. He may be John the Baptist, raised from the dead, or even the prophet Elijah. Jesus presses the question home: Who do the disciples think that he is? Simon Peter does not hesitate: Jesus is the messiah. Jesus does not say yes or no; he simply tells them not to tell anyone else. And then—this is the key for Mark—"he began to teach them that the Son of Man must suffer many things, and be rejected by the elders and the priests and the scribes, and be killed, and after three days rise again. And he said this plainly" (Mark 8:31–32). Peter bristles and actually condemns Jesus for saying this. Jesus bristles and condemns Peter for denying it; he even calls his friend "Satan," the tempter. So Jesus *seems to* assent to the title of messiah. He *seems to* give himself the title "Son of Man," a title that has a powerful biblical echo from the popular prophetic and apocalyptic book of Daniel (8:17). And then he *seems to* be given yet another title, in the very next chapter, when God identifies Jesus as his Son. Great prophet Elijah, John revived, Son of Man, Son of God—what can the accumulation of all these titles mean? Jesus has told them very plainly: it will mean suffering, suffering as the necessary prelude to saving. You've got to go down to rise up. None of his friends or followers ever seem to get this point, despite the fact that he said it all quite plainly.

Instead, the mission begins to fray around the edges, and the circle begins to come apart. The disciples are now caught squabbling with one another about who is favored, and who deserves what reward (Mark 10:35–45). Jesus is suddenly intent on going to Jerusalem; he's never been there before, since in Mark's gospel, he worked strictly in Galilee, in the north. When he finally does go south, Jesus goes out of his way to make trouble. He publicly condemns the hypocrisy of the Pharisees and Jerusalem priests, a *religious* act that clearly exacerbated his collision with Jewish officials. He drives the money changers out of the Temple complex (Mark 11:11–19), a *political* act that clearly led to his collision with the Roman civil administration. He dismisses the importance of the Jerusalem Temple when his disciples ask about it, and he dismisses overly simple imaginings of "the end of things," telling his disciples simply to watch, to wait, and to pay attention (in the so-called mini-Apocalypse at Mark 13:1–37).

They eat a last meal together; Jesus does not even make it to Passover. He is betrayed by one of his own, seized by a crowd in the late evening hours, arrested by the Romans, and crucified immediately. All of his followers have abandoned him; even the two men crucified alongside of him mock and berate Jesus (Mark 15:32). The defeat is total, the abandonment complete, and the scandal of it all almost unbearable. Jesus's last words are a quotation from one of King David's laments, the purest form of religious poetry that is also a shriek of despair: "My God, my God, why have you abandoned me?" (Mark 15:34; Psalms 22:18). The whole thing lasted barely a month.

Tragic Endings

"And immediately" is one of the most common transitional phrases in Mark's gospel. Some scholars have taken this as evidence that he did not know Greek very well, and there may be some truth to that.[18] But to emphasize the crudity of the phrasing is to miss the powerful economy in Mark's way of putting things. Every time Jesus does something or says something, he is gone "immediately." There is never enough time in Mark's gospel, never time to explain what has happened, to go over it again, to ask further questions. Jesus is dynamite: he came, he lit, it exploded. And—here is the tragic heart of Mark's message—what looked like the end was not the end. There is no end, in a tragedy.

Amazingly, Mark's gospel ends without a resurrection appearance either. In Mark's telling, the women go to the tomb where Jesus's body has been laid out in order to anoint it, to give it the ritual care they did not have time for when he was killed so suddenly. But the body is gone. A mysterious young man says that "he is not here," but has gone before them, back to Galilee. The women should go tell Peter this amazing news. But they run away "and tell no one, for they were afraid" (Mark 16:8). The first word of Mark's gospel was *beginning;* the last word is not *end,* because there is no end. Rather, the last word is *fear,* a tragic emotion that creates the possibility of a new kind of Christian compassion.

Many Christians find it impossible to accept the idea that Mark would end his gospel without a resurrection appearance. But that resistance may reflect a failure to understand some important aspects of Mark's gospel. All of the oldest manuscript copies of Mark's gospel end at 16:8, without a resurrection appearance by Jesus.[19] Mark clearly believes in Jesus's rising; in his own presentation of the gospel, Jesus himself predicted it plainly three times (Mark 8:31, 9:30–32, 10:33–34). But Mark also knows that anyone who wants to preach the resurrection will almost invariably fail to take the crucifixion seriously enough. Anyone who wants to be a martyr has failed to understand Mark's gospel message. People want to be either optimists or pessimists; Mark takes those options away, because he views them as false temptations. All there is the truth of this thing, the fact that "hard sayings" and "good news" are combined, the fact that a saving takes great suffering. Mark leaves us with one grimly hopeful fact: the women who were ordered to spread the word did not. But the very existence of Mark's gospel proves that the word did get out. So God simply found another way. What seems to be the end never really is, not if you are paying attention. Why did Mark tell his story this way? Why is his gospel structured as a tragedy? As I suggested at the end of the Chapter Two, I believe Mark's intention was to counter those Jews and Greeks who were making martyrdom the central message and the ascetic heart of this new religion.

It is instructive that later Christians, who had a taste of how explicit descriptions of Jesus's resurrection appearances made them feel, added one to Mark's gospel (we have seen how Luke's version left a lasting imprint, and Matthew's and John's versions have a similar feel to them). But what they added is, for lack of a better word, comical. It denies and turns upside down every hard truth Mark's Jesus has been at such pains to communicate, the very views he died defending. There are two alternative longer endings that were later attached to Mark's gospel, one of them only a single verse long, the other running to some eleven verses. The shorter ending simply says that the women changed their minds; they did report briefly to Peter, and then Jesus appeared to send them out. The longer ending is the comical one. In the beginning it is reminiscent of Luke's story, to which it clearly owes its general design. Jesus appears to Mary of Magdala first, then to two unnamed people on the road, and then to all eleven surviving disciples. He orders them to go out and to preach. He divides the world into saved people and condemned people; this is everyone's last chance. And the good news for the disciples is that they will be protected against all harm while they preach. If they are bitten by serpents, and even if they drink poison, they will remain unharmed. They can heal others just as surely as they can heal themselves ("Mark" 16:18). Later pagans, like Porphyry, a third-century Neoplatonist from Alexandria who clearly knew the New Testament very well, used this verse to devastating rhetorical effect. The best argument against a Christian, he mocks, is to dare the person to drink poison, as their Lord instructed.

It would be a laughable ending if it were not so very sad and such a monumental misrepresentation of Mark's beliefs. It is also blatantly untrue; many of the apostles were killed, after all. Mark's whole point has been that preaching and living and dying were not easy for Jesus; if those things were not easy for him, then they won't be easy for his followers either. Jesus's faith in God did not spare him any suffering at all. So far was Jesus from immunity to pain and death, Mark insists, that he depicts Jesus's death as virtually the most painful one imaginable. This is a gospel that will *not* take your pain or suffering away. Just the opposite, in fact; this gospel insists that you look directly at pain and suffering, taking the full measure of a broken world that has the capacity to break us, too. Mark's Jesus looks into that darkness, believing that the only light worth seeing is to be seen, just there. And everything, absolutely everything, follows from this. If you pay attention to human suffering, as tragedy demands that we do, then you will come to a comprehension of compassionate loving-kindness that is dramatically different from any you have known before. You would never celebrate the infliction of pain on another human being. You would never delight in the damning of the wicked. You would never again use the law to drive a wedge between you and your fellow citizens. You would accept the challenge to love God and to love your neighbor as a full-time job and a life's work. There is nothing else, for Mark's Jesus, than that; this mystery, of tragedy-informed love, provides the pulse beat of everything he wished ultimately to reveal.

Tragic Questions

One important and perhaps distressing question will have occurred to many readers who have made it to this point. It is a question that my brightest students frequently ask me whenever I teach this material. It is this: If the message of Mark's gospel is even half as provocative as I suggest it is, then how was it ever included in the Christian canon? This is a challenging question (it stymied me the first time I was asked), but several possible answers suggest themselves to the historically and archaeologically attuned modern reader.

First, it's possible that Mark's message may not have been as provocative to an ancient audience as it seems to us today. We today are troubled by many beliefs and practices, such as human enslavement, that did not trouble ancient people. It is conceivable that the story of Abraham's willingness to sacrifice his own son, Isaac (Genesis 22:1–19), would not have been as troubling to an early Bronze Age audience as it is to us today. Ancient attitudes are simply different from modern attitudes; the ancients were untroubled by things that trouble us—and vice versa. Moreover, Mark's audience confronted problems most modern Western Christians do not, such as the possibility of martyrdom and the impending war with Rome. The point I am making here is the point I emphasized at the beginning of the book: that archaeology provides the root metaphor for our modern endeavors in Christian reading, a metaphor that may help us recognize that modern attitudes are often distinct and that we are inescapably modern people. Our reading of the gospels will reflect this, whether we are conscious of it or not. It is better by far to be conscious of it.

A second answer is related to the first one. It may be that the gospel message Mark imagined seems more troubling to us because we are aware of what later writers did with it. Later New Testament authors seem to have gone out of their way to answer questions that Mark posed and left unanswered. This is the same strategy that led them to rewrite Mark's ending, and to do it so poorly. So now, if we read Mark's gospel through the interpretive lens provided by Matthew or by Luke, it may well seem much stranger to us. And as I will suggest in the next chapter, if we read Mark's gospel through the interpretive lens provided by John, then it can seem downright impossible. But it is extremely important to remember that *Mark's gospel came first.*

A third answer to this crucial canonical question involves thinking more specifically about who Mark's audience was when he wrote his gospel. If, as I believe was the case, Mark's audience (and indeed, the audience for all three Synoptic gospels) was a Greek audience and not a Jewish one, then aspects of his story may have seemed less troubling. Framing the story of Jesus's life and death as a tragedy would not have been shocking or repellant to such an audience, even if the idea seems strange to most modern Christians today. Nor would the idea that a person could be a "son of God" seem strange. I'll turn to that important point again in the next chapter. But before doing so, another aspect of the different audiences that Mark and John had in mind is important to mention. I alluded to it already in the story I told in Chapter Two.

It seems likely that Mark's gospel was written for people who were already converts to this new faith and who therefore already knew a fair amount about the story of Jesus—about who he was, what he said, and how he died. Much like a classical Greek audience that went to the theater, not to learn what was going to happen to Oedipus (they already knew that), but rather to see how this particular tragedian would tell the tale, some Greek converts to this new religious movement may have been drawn to the power of the way in which Mark (and Mark's Jesus) made things come about.[20] This marks one of the crucial differences between Mark and John. Alone among the four canonical stories, what I am calling John's evangel was evangelical in the literal sense, designed for people who had *not* heard Jesus's story before. That difference in the writer's intended audience makes all the difference, and

I suspect that it helps explain why John's gospel is still the one most often used for "evangelical" purposes today.

Having come to this point in my thinking about how to answer a very good and very difficult question, I wish now to turn the question upside down, in order to answer it anew in the next chapter. Why, I wonder, do we ask this question of Mark's gospel but do not ask it of John's evangel? The whole purpose of this book is to point out just how radical the challenge to Christians that is embodied in Mark's gospel really is—not to make Mark's gospel seem strange, but rather to make John's evangel seem stranger. For the fact is that in the early centuries of Christian formation, the question Christians puzzled over was not whether Mark should be included in the canon, but whether John should be. John's evangel was far more shocking to ancient audiences. Here once again, we modern people must work very carefully, with more finely developed historical habits, to be able to feel the shock that John's evangel might have created in an ancient Christian audience that knew and admired Mark's version. The power of Mark's performance has something to do with Jesus's passionate humanity, something to do with compassion in the face of unimaginable suffering, and it has everything to do with tragedy. John turned all of this upside down by writing an anti-tragic evangel in which Jesus's humanity is muted and all compassion, much like the wavering disciples, has fled.

CHAPTER FOUR

From Tragedy to Triumph

John Against Mark

We read but do not write tragedies. The tragic solution of the problem of existence, the reconciliation to life by means of the tragic spirit is, that is to say, now only a fiction surviving in art. When that art has become, as it probably will, completely meaningless, when we have ceased not only to write but to read tragic works, then it will be lost and in all real senses forgotten, since the devolution from Religion to Art to Document will be complete.

—JOSEPH WOOD KRUTCH, *THE MODERN TEMPER* (1929)

I n the fireside story I recounted in Chapter Two, I imagined John as a younger and somewhat wide-eyed listener to the virtuoso gospel performances of Luke and Matthew and Mark. Mark's version of Gethsemane, I suggested, would have turned the most heads. It clearly turned John's, so much so that he decided to take on Mark's gospel directly, to turn it around, and then to supplant it with his own very different story.

John's differences from Mark are clear from the very beginning, and they increase as his story progresses. The question is whether that was accidental (because he did not know Mark's story) or by design (because he did). I have suggested that it was deliberate, and in the garden at Gethsemane,

I think it clearly was. Now, the question of whether John knew Mark's gospel at all has been hotly debated by modern biblical scholars (it was already a question in antiquity). Ever since the groundbreaking work by David Friedrich Strauss (1808–1874) on the historical Jesus[1] (bitterly criticized by later scholars from Friedrich Nietzsche to Albert Schweitzer),[2] scholars have generally agreed that Mark's chronology and John's can't both be true. And most all modern biblical scholars (with the important exception of E. R. Goodenough and William Albright[3]) assumed that John's gospel was written considerably later than Mark's—so John was dependent on Mark, and not the other way around. In the United States, a lesser-known transitional figure from Yale University by the name of Benjamin Wisner Bacon (1860–1932) summarized the current state of this scholarship by noting that John's gospel (before the Second World War, scholars still thought all four versions functioned similarly as "gospels") "reproduces that of Mark as modified by Luke,"[4] though toward the end of his life he modified that view.[5] (Notice once again how determinative Luke's version became for subsequent Christian storytellers.) Shortly after Bacon's death, another prominent biblical scholar, P. Gardner-Smith, suggested that it might be easier to make sense of John's gospel if we assumed that he did not know Mark's (or the other Synoptic gospels) at all.[6] And then came the postwar discoveries of new religious manuscripts at Qumran and Nag Hammadi, and the whole game shifted, much as I have already described. For my purposes, I assume that John knew Mark's story, but how I imagine that kind of "story" and that kind of "knowing" involves a dramatic analogy, the way one can be familiar with a story without ever actually reading it. I simply assume that John knew the rough itinerary of Mark's Jesus and that he assuredly knew the story of a troubled prayer in a private place near the end of Jesus's life. What John clearly didn't know anything about was tragedy.

In fact, it's by reexamining what we learned about Greek tragedy, with Hegel's and Nietzsche's help, that we can see just how different John's evangelical vision is from Mark's more authentically tragic one. Remember that Hegel saw tragedy fundamentally as a collision of wills, as well as an exploration of the new ethical and political possibilities such collisions create. In John's evangel, all the collisions are horizontal, most of them between Jesus and "the Jews," and they have a rather unsatisfying, know-it-all quality to them. Far different from Hegel's readings, these really are depicted as conflicts between good and evil, not between two forms of good, since the Jews are given no good arguments on their side. Whereas in Mark's gospel, everything is left half in the dark, in John's evangel, Jesus knows everything, is everything, and explains everything very clearly; people are simply too dumb or too duplicitous to accept what he says. Hence he is in conflict with almost everyone, save a very select few, like John himself. John's Jesus cannot experience a tragedy in the vertical dimension because that would bring him into collision with God's will, and given the radical new way in which John imagines Jesus, that is theoretically impossible. Mark's Gethsemane is theoretically impossible for John. Jesus's will and God's will are in perfect alignment; that is why John simply cannot imagine or tell the story of the Gethsemane prayer that Mark made so central and so poignant.

Nietzsche helps us see something else of importance as well. Recall that Nietzsche believed that tragedy was born of the Greeks' ability to keep their eyes fixed on the great darkness until they began to see flashes of light and insight. John plays expertly with the imagery of lightness and darkness in his evangel, but here once again, he does so in an utterly untragic way. The world is divided between the powers of light and darkness, John believes. Most of the world is mired in a darkness so complete that it cannot see Jesus for who he truly is. Jesus, by contrast, is pure light, but the vast majority of human beings on whom his light shines will be unsuited to accept it. This failure is their fault, and so in John's evangel, the emotional response of damning judgment gradually replaces that of tragic compassion. Since Jesus is light, he (and John) cannot believe that anything positive comes from darkness. As we have seen, Mark believed just the opposite. John has no use for language or ideas like Mark's. Here, then, is what John seems to have made of Mark's gospel instead.

From Gospel to Evangel

John's evangel begins with what appears to have been an early Christian prayer or song[7] that explains that Jesus is the *Logos* of God (John 1:1–5):

> In the beginning was the *logos*
> and the *logos* was with God
> and the *logos* was God.

This *logos* was in the beginning with God.
Everything came to be through him,
and not a single thing came to be without him.
Every thing that came to be was life in him,
and life was the light of humanity.
The light appeared in the darkness,
and the darkness did not understand it.

We have already discussed this ambitious and ambiguous Greek word, *Logos*. John immediately tells us, however, that the darkness that threatens this light cannot overcome it; that is a shockingly different message from the story Mark and the other Synoptic gospels tell, a story that culminates tragically in Gethsemane and scandalously on a cross. The rest of John's evangel will make the purpose of this poem abundantly clear. Jesus does not submit to the power of darkness in John's evangel; he simply takes his light with him and returns to its source.

The differences between a tragic gospel and an anti-tragic evangel are clear from the beginning, but it is the middle of John's evangel that really detonates the contrast between the two. John's Jesus actually mocks Mark's Gethsemane prayer midway through his evangel (John 12:27–28) and then once again near the end. And that mocking disagreement is tied directly to the way John's story ends: a resigned and triumphant Jesus says "it is finished" (a single Greek word, *tetelesthai*; John 19:30) as he expires, with no emotional sense of God's abandonment or physical pain. John, rather than Peter, proves to be the most faithful steward when it comes to acknowledging Jesus's rising (John 20:3–4); and this same John, the "beloved disciple," tells us that he has been an eyewitness to everything that is reported here (John 21:24). John is deliberately supplanting Peter's authority, Thomas's authority,[8] Mary's authority,[9] and, I am suggesting, the Synoptic authority of writers like Mark as well. John is not so subtly tying his own authority directly to that of Jesus, in a way that Mark warns us is tragically misguided and self-deluded. Now, if John's authority is connected to Jesus, and if Jesus's authority is tied to God, well then, how could you ever argue with John? The complex creative poem at the beginning of John's evangel turns increasingly aggressive as his story unfolds. I suppose we've all met at least one Christian evangelist who operates in this same way—all sweetness and light at the beginning, with authoritative judgment coming later, in the end.

Like Mark, but unlike Matthew and Luke, John begins with Jesus's baptism, not his childhood. Unlike Mark, John tells us that the Baptist clearly and publicly indicated that Jesus was the messiah (John 1:19–23). John the Baptist himself says so, identifying Jesus as "the Lamb of God, who takes away the sins of the world" (John 1:29). That image will become far more important in the end.

Immediately after his baptism, Jesus calls his disciples, but unlike Mark's disciples, they all recognize Jesus as the messiah too (John 1:41, 45). Next, Jesus performs his very first miracle, turning water into wine at a wedding in Cana, a small town where Jesus spends a great deal of time in John's evangel (John 2:1–11). There is no temptation of this Jesus; he is not really human, and as such, he is already far beyond any possibility of temptation. Jesus's soul can never be torn asunder. So instead of wandering in the desert alone, John's Jesus makes the first of many trips to Jerusalem, and in his very *first* public act there, he provokes everyone: he fashions a knotted whip for himself and uses this scourge to drive the money changers violently from the portico of the Jerusalem Temple (John 2:13–22). According to Mark, this was Jesus's last public act before his betrayal and arrest. For a man like John, Mark's ending is only the beginning.

Most of the stories in this portion of John's evangel are unique to him. There is, for instance, the story of Jesus's famous conversation with Nicodemus, a Jewish leader in Jerusalem. That conversation culminates in what is perhaps the most commonly cited of all New Testament verses, omnipresently displayed on television every time a football team kicks an extra point: "For God loved the world so much that he gave the only-begotten Son, so that all who believe in him should not be lost but have life forever" (John 3:16). What is telling is that so few Christians acknowledge the lines that come next, for they are the key to understanding the hard lines, and the hard message, of John's evangel:

> God did not send the Son into the world to condemn it, but rather so that the world might be saved through him. He who believes in him is not condemned; *he who does not believe is condemned already,* since he has not believed in the name of the only begotten Son of God. *And this is the judgment: the light has come into the world, and people loved darkness more than the light, because their deeds were evil* [John 3:17–19, italics mine].

The emphasis in this passage is on the evil of people and their condemnation by God, not on compassionate love (see

John 2:24–25 for another example of this same argument). There is even the hint of a suggestion, one that John's Jesus will develop later on (John 6:64–65, 8:20, 8:44–47, 18:4), that this is all foreordained, that the choice of who is saved and who is lost was made before the believers themselves were born. Remember what John told us in the beginning: before people were created, there was *Logos* and light; the light has come into the world, and the darkness cannot touch it. But now we are told that "men" love darkness rather than light. Clearly, then, men cannot touch the divine light, and Jesus will take it with him when he goes. Jesus wins even if no one understands or accepts him; most will not. But that is their loss, not God's.

Chapter 4 provides another story unique to John's evangel. Jesus happens upon an anonymous woman from Samaria, a region in central Palestine that Jews from other regions—Judea in the south, Galilee in the north—loved to look down on (that's the whole point of the Synoptic parable about the "good Samaritan," by the way: in biblical times, *no one* thought a Samaritan could be good). The woman freely acknowledges that Jesus is a prophet. Then she asks him about the right place to worship God. People from Jerusalem insist that their Temple is the most sacred place in the Jewish world and insist that Jews from other places, like Samaria, must make pilgrimage there to worship properly. She wonders if that's right, since there are even older Jewish temples in her part of the world. Jesus's answer is mysterious; he tells her that the days are coming when people will not worship in temples like these at all. "You worship what you do not know; we worship what we know, since salvation is from the Jews" (John 4:22).

This is another commonly quoted verse, of course, but it is also misrepresented and misunderstood by most who quote it. As the woman's questions make clear, Jesus was not talking about "Jews"; he was talking about Judeans. He was not saying that the messiah had to be Jewish; everyone is Jewish in this story. Rather, he was saying that the saving event will come from Judea, the region immediately to the south of this woman's homeland. And it will be a saving that has nothing at all to do with temples (Jesus has already attacked the Temple) but with a person. The woman apparently knows this too; Jesus is clearly talking about the messiah. "I know that the messiah is coming, the one called *christos;* when he comes, he will show us everything" (John 4:25), she says. John's Jesus pulls no punches. He always speaks freely and clearly, offering people a once-and-for-all lifetime chance. The time is at hand, he informs her; *he* is this messiah. John later tells us that people at the time confused the matter by worrying that Jesus did not really come from Judea (John 7:40–44), which is why his saying that "salvation is from Judea" is so important.

Immediately thereafter, Jesus returns to Jerusalem (which is in Judea, of course) for yet another religious festival. He does this a great deal in John's evangel, though John regularly refers to them as "feasts of the Jews," almost as if Jesus were no longer Jewish himself. John's Jesus transcends such categories. Now Jesus's open and public proclamations on his own behalf begin to become even more elevated and to shock the traditional religious sensibilities of first-century Judaism. Not content with claiming to be the messiah, Jesus begins to refer to God as his own father, implicitly "making himself equal to God"

(John 5:18). That is the claim—a claim that accelerates and expands ever more outrageously in the rest of this evangel—that will prevent most Jews from believing or honoring what Jesus says. His words are not light; they are strange-sounding and heretical. One of the many unique qualities of John's evangel is the way he refers to "Jews" as a people with whom he shares no attachment. Even Jesus seems completely alienated from them. This kind of rhetoric bore a bitter harvest centuries later, when Christians came to power and exerted that power against, well, everyone else—but especially against Jews and Greeks.

The dramatically un-Markan and anti-tragic flow of this evangel increases in pace and in tone. In chapter 6, Jesus remains in Galilee for the Passover. He miraculously feeds five thousand people, and those people, convinced of his power and authority, wish to make him their king. So Jesus withdraws. But among his more immediate circle of followers, Jesus explains the symbolic value of this feeding miracle. "I am the bread of life; whoever comes to me shall no longer hunger, and whoever believes in me shall never thirst again" (John 6:35). That some Christians would take this verse as a promise is but one part of the larger comedy of John's evangelical legacy. John's inability to conceive of Jesus tragically created theological mayhem later on. This is as farcical a promise as the one in the false ending to Mark's gospel (which owes its structure to the end of John's evangel, by the way), the nonsense promise that Christians will not suffer hunger, or thirst, or anything worse. Of course they did. Jesus himself did; Christians still do. Then comes the final outrage. John's Jesus tells his followers that they must eat his body and drink his blood in order to be satiated forever (John 6:53–59). That, ironically enough, is the last straw for many of his own disciples; it is a pronouncement so weird that it is too hard for them to bear (John 6:60), and many of them stop following Jesus because of it (John 6:66). There is even a hint that this statement is what decided Judas on betraying him (John 6:71, although later, blame is placed squarely on Satan, at John 13:2, yet Satan's work was ironically enabled by Jesus's own powers at John 13:27–30).

Next comes the Feast of Tabernacles in chapter 7, and Jesus returns once again to Jerusalem. At first, he had opted not to go and sent his disciples in his place (John 7:8–9). After their departure however, Jesus comes on his own, in secret (John 7:10). Strangely, after all of this secrecy, once he gets to the city, Jesus appears quite publicly in the Temple, and his message is now aimed strictly at broadcasting his own authority. His authority, he tells the crowd, just *is* God's authority (John 7:14–24). And now, for some reason, those who object most emphatically to what he is saying are those most afraid to go anywhere near him. If Jesus is growing in authority, he is also becoming more and more terrifying, more and more distant and untouchable.

The next story John tells would seem to undercut the point just made in the Temple. It is one of the most famous of all John's stories, the tale of an anonymous woman taken in adultery and of Jesus's saving her by inviting "the one without sin to cast the first stone" at her (John 8:7). In fact, as Bart Ehrman has shown convincingly,[10] this story, like the longer ending of Mark's gospel, was added later. It is far too compassionate to square with the portrait of Jesus John has painted thus far, and in any case, the narrative flow of this gospel makes more sense if we move from the end of chapter 7 straight to John 8:12.[11]

Jesus now begins to preach with a repetitive phrase that he will use throughout the rest of this evangel: "I am." We already met that phrase twice in John's version of Gethsemane. *Egô eimi* is a Greek phrase that is a conscious echo of the most holy revelation of the divine name to Moses, revealed just before he was sent to Egypt to deliver the Israelites from their bondage (Exodus 4:13–14). God initially identified himself as "the God of Abraham, Isaac, and Jacob," but Moses presses him for another name. God's reply, *Yahweh,* is mysterious, and although scholars debate what this name actually meant, it is built on the root for the Hebrew verb *to be* and thus suggests something like "I am who I am" or "I will be who I will be." The Dead Sea Scrolls indicate that this name was deemed so holy by some Jews a generation before Jesus's day that they would not even write the letters down; Jewish scribes simply placed four dots in the scroll to indicate the presence of the divine name. John's Jesus adapts this sacred name to his own purposes, too. He is free to use it, free to say it. In fact, Jesus now speaks as if he were God. "I am the light of the world" (John 8:12), he says. There is none of the tragic darkness that plagued Mark's gospel, lent it its mystery, and yet also made his portrait of Jesus work. "I am from above" (John 8:23), he says. And in so saying, he suggests that things here below, on earth, do not have real value or consequence. This otherworldliness will be intensified at the end of John's evangel, as we saw when John's Jesus adamantly rejected the Gethsemane prayer. His kingdom "is not of this world," he insists. "If my kingdom were of this world, then my followers would fight" (John 18:36). In any case, these are the claims—making a man equal to the God of Abraham, and making things of this world seem irrelevant—that traditional Jews simply could not accept. But what is Jesus's reaction to their perfectly understandable concerns? He radicalizes his message even further, almost as if he is trying to alienate them completely, trying to turn them away: "Truly, truly, I say to you, before Abraham was, *I am*" (John 8:58).

Many biblical scholars now believe that the original inspiration for the composition of John's evangel was the fact that Jesus's followers had recently been kicked out of their synagogues, right around the time when they started calling themselves "Christians." Presumably, some of the things they were saying about Jesus were deemed blasphemous by more tradition-minded Jews. Chapter 9 of John's evangel may be read virtually as a transcript of how these debates played out and the predictable results. Christians have all the best lines, but Jews have all the power. It is prompted by what is undoubtedly Jesus's strangest miracle. He makes a sort of paste out of dirt and his own spittle and places this poultice on the eyes of a blind man, whose sight is thereby restored (we can see John's fingerprints, not Jesus's, in this clay!). The man's blindness makes him a pretty easy symbol for everyone in the world who walks in darkness until Jesus brings them light. But he is also a symbol of the Deuteronomic debates then swirling in many Jewish synagogues. Some people think that his blindness must be a punishment from God; or else, given that he has been blind since birth, it must be a punishment aimed at his parents; or else it is a symbol of "original sin." Jesus makes short work of such religious reasoning. But the rabbis are unrelenting. They condemn Jesus for healing on the Sabbath and claim that he must be in league with evil forces. The now-sighted man insists on Jesus's goodness. The rabbis retort that since the man has clearly been in sin since his birth, he is in no position to judge such matters. And when he insists that he can, they drive him out of the synagogue. Such debates are never far from John's mind. But so is his ever-present quarrel with Mark.

There comes yet another holiday, the Feast of Dedication this time, and once again Jesus returns to Jerusalem. It is winter now. The Jerusalem Jews ask him to speak plainly, to tell them clearly if he is the messiah. Jesus is in no mood to be forgiving. He has already told them in no uncertain terms that he is the messiah; they are simply incapable of believing it (John 10:24–25). We know what this means for John. They are condemned; in fact, their condemnation is part of God's plan. Amazingly, Jesus goes out of his way to outrage and alienate them still further. His next saying is the most shocking one of all: "I and the Father are one" (John 10:30). That statement, so deliberately outrageous to traditional Jewish sensibilities, triggers a fairly predictable reaction; the crowd wishes to stone him. Jesus deflects this threat in a very interesting way, according to John: he uses the scriptures. Jesus has already explained that the title "Son of Man" is appropriately biblical (John 9:35–41). Now he demonstrates that this new title, "Son of God," is also quite traditional; King David himself used it and invited us to do so as well

(John 10:32–38). Jesus manages to escape the clutches of the crowd (John doesn't bother to tell us how), and in escaping, he has avoided the obvious question. The problem is not in claiming to be messiah or Son of Man or even Son of God. The problem is with the claim to be equal to God.

In chapter 11, John resolves that problem in an interesting way, with another story that is unique to his evangel. Jesus retreats to the neighborhood of Bethany, and while he is there, he actually raises a man named Lazarus from death. Hearing this, the entire Jerusalem community is now resolved to kill him (John 11:53), so Jesus no longer travels openly in that city (John 11:54).

But eventually he does return, for a final and definitive visit. It is Passover again, the third one in John's evangel, and thus the third year of Jesus's public ministry. Jesus returns from where he and his disciples have been hiding out (in a place called Ephraim; John 11:54), and he stays with Lazarus's family in Bethany. He is resolved now to return to Jerusalem, to die there. Whereas Mark's Jesus did not quite make it to Passover, John's Jesus does. The reason is rather simple: John's Jesus is himself the Paschal "Lamb of God," just as John the Baptist said he was, the sacrificial being whose death will set things right again. John's God still requires sacrifices, apparently, and a human one at that. It is precisely here that John's wholesale rejection of Mark's gospel message becomes clearest. John's Jesus actually makes fun of what is arguably the most poignant moment in Mark's gospel, Jesus's anguished prayer in Gethsemane: "Now is my soul troubled. And what shall I say? 'Father, save me from this hour?' No, for this purpose I have come to this hour. Father, glorify your name" (John 12:27–28).

If we take seriously what John has told us so far, then something very strange is happening here, something cosmic in its significance, something that will draw a fundamental line through the rest of human history, between those who see and those who do not. There is no blurring of light and darkness in John's evangel. You are saved or you are condemned, and it can happen in an instant. God will glorify God's own name, which is also Jesus's name, and because of this, there can be no Passion, no Gethsemane, no doubt, and no despair. As we saw in chapter 1, the only reason that John's Jesus is crucified at all is because he himself makes it happen, forces the crowd to do what they are afraid to do unprompted. This is not just the story of the death of God's Son, the Incarnate Word of God; this story has mapped out the death of Christian compassion as well. Mark warned us against drawing lines. Mark warned us that no one sees everything clearly, not even Jesus. Rather, light and dark are intertwined in every human life. The appropriate response to these tragic realities are pity and fear and compassion. For John, by contrast, the end of the matter is judgment.

Turning Against the World

Near the end of John's evangel, right after Jesus's refusal to pray in the garden, John's story takes some further comic twists and anti-tragic turns. If Jesus's soul cannot be divided, if he cannot ever doubt, and if Jesus knows the future and knows that he has come to earth to die on a cross, then John simply cannot write a Passion narrative with the kind of poignancy, terror, or grief that Mark managed so brilliantly.

So according to John, after Jesus is arrested in the garden, he is brought before the Roman provincial governor, Pilate, who is very ambivalent about the arrest. Pilate is a cynic; he famously asks Jesus, "What is truth?" (John 18:38), since he knows that so many people who come to him with charges and countercharges cannot all be telling the truth (and presumably, none of them are). What is strange is that this Roman who trusts no one to tell the truth seems to have such genuine sympathy for Jesus, the ultimate truth teller, and does not think he should be killed (John 18:28–19:16). John's evangel places the blame for Jesus's death squarely on (who else?) "the Jews." Jesus is flogged, but John mentions this casually, almost in passing, in a single verse (John 19:1). Instead of a close description of his awful, tragic suffering as we saw in Mark, John focuses on the backstory, a long debate between the Roman governor, Pilate, and "the Jews." As in the garden, so too now at the end: Jesus remains in full control and never wavers; the rest of the world has no idea what is truly going on. Jesus carries his own cross without assistance (John 19:17). He is identified, correctly if ironically, as "the King of the Jews" by Pilate, much to the consternation of those same Jews (John 19:20–22). He asks for wine, drinks it calmly, and then gives up the ghost with what in Greek is a single word: "It is finished" (John 19:30). Only John reports Jesus's last words this way.[12] John's Jesus has completed his mission, done all that he came to do, and now he presumably returns to the divine light from whence he came.

Without a doubt the oddest story John tells involves him personally. In John's evangel, there is no interaction between Jesus and the two men who were crucified with him. Recall that in Mark's gospel, even they mocked Jesus (Mark 15:32). In Luke's gospel, one of the two men came to believe Jesus, and Jesus promised him paradise (Luke 23:39–43). Even when he is dying on a cross, John's Jesus focuses his attention on two other people, but not the two criminals, who are presumably already lost. No, Jesus is focused on his mother and "the disciple whom he loved" (John 19:26). He tells them to belong to one another, and the disciple, "from that very hour," took Mary, the mother of Jesus, into his own home (John 19:27). Later we learn that this "beloved disciple" was none other than John himself (John 21:24). Now *that* is one way to claim authority among the later followers of Jesus!

Authority Again

The fundamental irony of this man who dubbed himself the "beloved disciple" is that he does not seem to love anybody else, except Jesus. John helps establish a trend that will characterize a great deal of Christian activity in the first four centuries after Jesus's scandalous execution. He fights on multiple fronts; military images dominate his thinking and his rhetoric. This evangel describes a cosmic battle between light and darkness. John, as we have already seen in great detail, is opposed to Jews, almost all Jews, excepting those few and rather unusual ones who were not offended by a man who "equated himself with God." John's evangel is an extended polemic against Jews who, in his severe judgment, saw Jesus in all his glory, heard him at first hand clearly explain who he was, and yet still refused to believe in him and what he promised. For such people, only darkness and condemnation are left. But John is also opposed to nearly all of the other potential authority figures among the early followers of Jesus. If the noncanonical gospel of Thomas was as popular as the Nag Hammadi collection and subsequent commentaries suggest that it was, and if "Didymus Judas Thomas" was believed to have been Jesus's twin, then John is clearly interested in supplanting Thomas's authority with his own. Gregory Riley and Elaine Pagels have both written elegant analyses of this anti-Thomas dimension of John's evangel.[13] It is most clearly evident in the famous story told about Jesus's rising, at which point John invents one of the most memorable of all canonical characters: the "doubting Thomas."[14] Thomas, we are told, was excluded from Jesus's first visit to all his other disciples after his rising; he did not see Jesus risen until eight days later (John 20:24–29). And when he finally did see Jesus, Thomas refused to believe his own eyes. He insisted on touching Jesus's body, more specifically, on touching his *wounds.* The moral of this story cuts to the heart of Thomas's authority and wisdom: "Have you believed because you have seen me?" Jesus frowns. "Blessed are those who have not seen and yet believe" (John 20:29). The beloved disciple would never be subject to such a charge. He alone of all the disciples is described in this way: "He saw *and* he believed" (John 20:8). Period. Now John insists on the same fast faith from his own readers and disciples.

John is clearly hard at work to establish his authority against Peter as well. According to John, he alone anticipated Jesus's betrayal, and he alone actually asked Jesus about it directly at the last meal they shared together (John 21:20). Later, when the women give the disciples their shocking news of Jesus's disappearance from the tomb, Peter and John sprint off immediately to see it for themselves. John wins the race, literally and figuratively, getting to the tomb before Peter does (John 20:1–3). John—that is to say, best loved by Jesus, the closest and the fastest and the most faithful—has clearly surpassed all the rest.

His desire by now seems very clear: John wishes to become the one and only evangelist. Monotheists should be monoevangelicals, in his fervent opinion. In a world of darkness, there is precious little light. John believes he has that light (small wonder that some Gnostics were inclined to John's vision and his evangel, as we will see in the next chapter). And yet as Mark knew well, the crucifixion was a very great darkness, for Jesus and for his friends. Christian light may be found only there, very close to that tragic pain and suffering.

Hostile as John was to "the Jews," he seems surprisingly uneasy about "the Greeks" as well (see John 7:32–36). And much as John sought to outrank Thomas and Peter, he sought to replace Mark outright. I am suggesting that these stances are linked, that John opposed Mark not only because of his long affiliation with Peter, but also because of the sheer Greekness, the tragic quality, of Mark's gospel. The trouble for Christians after John will be this: How can you venerate a human Jesus once you have imagined and worshiped him as divine? And how can you take the crucifixion seriously if you know that he was raised up later and all was well? As I demonstrated in Chapter Three, Mark went to extraordinary lengths to hang on to this tension and found some remarkably poetic ways to do so, most of them inspired by tragedy. In Mark's gospel, we do not know what Jesus is, and we're not supposed to. His gospel ends without a resurrection appearance precisely so that we will admit to the terror of what came before. John changes all of that, virtually point for point. And that fundamental opposition, the two roads that branched out from John's anti-tragic decision to deny Mark's Gethsemane prayer, created the primary set of problems that Christians would devote the next several centuries to trying to resolve. How can you have Mark's gospel and John's evangel both? How can Jesus be both a human being who died in despair on a cross and the Incarnate *Logos* who created the universe and all the people in it? Attempts to answer these questions were destined to result in the deliciously paradoxical formula Christians recite as the Nicene Creed.

I will turn to some of the wonderfully supple moves that early Christian theologians made in their attempts to hold Mark's vision and John's together, but first let me tie up some of the loose strands that I have tried to disentangle in this chapter. Mark wrote Jesus's story and imagined it as a tragedy, just one generation after Jesus's execution in Jerusalem. Gethsemane was the pivot on which Mark's understanding of the meaning of that whole story hinged. A generation after Mark's remarkable invention of the gospel, John wrote his evangel, as a deliberate attempt to turn Mark's genre upside down and to usurp his place at the center of Christian evangelism. John flatly denied

Mark's Gethsemane prayer—or rather, John insisted that Jesus did so—and thus John unwittingly wreaked havoc on Mark's conception of Christian compassion and the "Christian way." John's otherworldliness spoke most compellingly to a certain conception of martyrdom, insisting that Christianity is most successful and truest to itself when it is hated by the world—and in being hated, it conquers.[15]

Three and four generations further down this tangled Christian road, a great many other Christian communities wrote gospels, accounts that quarreled explicitly with one another and offered very different interpretations of who Jesus was and what his central message meant. By the year 200 C.E., this proliferation of gospels had reached the point where some way of ordering the chaos was needed. Several archaeological discoveries immediately after the Second World War have helped bring these issues more clearly into the light. I will turn to this rich and fascinating material in the next chapter.

CHAPTER FIVE

Secret Caves and Secret Teachings

The Shaping of Christian Orthodoxy

Whoever finds the interpretation of these sayings will not taste death.

—GOSPEL OF THOMAS, SEC. I

By the end of the first century, fully two generations after the death of Jesus, the tradition of writing "gospel" accounts of who different communities thought he was, and what the significance of his earthly ministry had been, became commonplace. If anything, it was this very proliferation of gospels that was destined to create severe tensions in this new religious movement, though we see evidence of this problem already in Paul's letters (most famously at 2 Corinthians 1:12–7:16). Apparently, lots of people claiming to be Christian were wandering around the eastern Mediterranean preaching messages that were so varied that they couldn't possibly all be right (could they be?) because they couldn't all be made to hang together. Either Jesus prayed for deliverance in Gethsemane, or else he refused that prayer.

You need to choose whether to believe Mark's version or John's. The real question thus rather quickly turned on the question of authority—not Jesus's authority this time so much as that of the gospel writers themselves. Who was in a position to distinguish sound doctrine from unsound doctrine, and who could say that the period of writing gospels should now come to a close? When should we move from writing new gospels to writing commentaries about the gospels we already have? After all, if Mark could write a gospel forty years after Jesus's disappearance, and if John could write a very different story some thirty years after Mark, then what is to stop me from writing a gospel too? If the door on the canon has been reopened, how are we ever to close it again?

The period immediately after the creation of John's evangel—roughly the years between 100 and 250 C.E., the second great period of mystery in early Christian studies—seems to be the period of the greatest proliferation of alternative gospels and Gnostic "secret books." This very proliferation is presumably what prompted the "orthodox" reaction later on, the sorts of heresy hunting designed to establish the canonical list of acceptable Christian writings, as well as some sense of the doctrines that make them sound or unsound.

We can say this and see it far more clearly today because in 1945 a hidden cache of twelve leather-bound codices buried in ceramic containers was discovered in the Egyptian desert near an oasis called Nag Hammadi; this is the so-called Nag Hammadi Library, discovered quite by accident by a local man named Muhammad Ali and his brother Khalifah. The Nag Hammadi Library suggests that the early followers of Jesus in the first several generations after his death spoke with an astonishing range of voices, and believed an astonishing variety of things, all of them grounded in an astonishing variety of authoritative figures these various communities held up as their leaders.

The Great Dispersion

One problem that bedeviled efforts to distinguish sound from unsound gospels, strangely enough, was the very common ancient practice of writing texts in other, more famous persons' names. The easiest way to authorize a would-be gospel, after all, was to claim that it was authored by an eyewitness or close follower of Jesus. Better still was to claim authorship by one of the very closest disciples who had received personal and private, and often secret, instruction from Jesus himself.

It is striking that not all the canonical gospels do this; they did not seem to feel the need to do so. Not yet. For instance, we do not know who Mark was. Perhaps he means us to understand that he is the young man who abandoned Jesus after Gethsemane; perhaps he means us to see him as the Roman centurion who understood Jesus to be the Son of God when he died (and not, be sure to note, when he rose up). Some later church traditions associated him with a man we meet in Acts of the Apostles named John Mark (Acts 12:12–25, but see also 15:36–41), but there is no inner evidence in Mark's gospel to suggest this connection. Other church traditions claim that Mark was a disciple of Peter and thus one generation removed from Jesus.[1] Matthew, by contrast, claims to be the eyewitness account of a disciple specially called by Jesus (Matthew 9:9, 10:3), but Matthew does not claim any special proximity or access to Jesus for himself. Just the opposite, in fact. Matthew tells us that he did not even join the movement until after the Sermon on the Mount and that Peter played the really crucial role throughout Jesus's ministry (Matthew 16:18–19). Luke similarly does not tell us who he was, though later church traditions associated him with Paul's ministry to the Greeks, much as Mark was associated with Peter. (As I have demonstrated, Luke was the most fluent in the Greek language and the most familiar with Greek literature, history, and philosophy.)[2]

It was John, and only John among the canonical evangelists, who explicitly identified himself as the man who was in a position to supplant everyone else's authority: he tells us in no uncertain terms that he was the most beloved disciple, so "beloved," in fact, that Jesus, dying on the cross, ordered John and his mother to belong to one another after his death (John 19:26–27). John's evangel is carefully choreographed to establish his authority over Peter, and Thomas, and Mary, all of whom seem to be his main rivals. And John concludes his evangel by emphasizing the fact that he was an eyewitness to everything he has reported (John 21:24, though there is strong textual evidence to suggest that this chapter was added later); he is the only New Testament writer who claims that.[3]

The problem is this: once someone decides to authorize his or her text in this way, and to supplant the authority of other texts in so doing, then anyone else can try the same thing. Most of the Christian documents discovered at Nag Hammadi and elsewhere do this, claiming authorship by an eyewitness follower of Jesus and the possession of some "secret" teachings given by Jesus in private conversation to that person alone (or at least as properly understood by that person alone and presumably misrepresented by everyone else). We can imagine how maddening this must have been to Christians who felt that the message of such gospels was suspect (Paul himself "raves" about this problem at 2 Corinthians 6:4–12). But they had only John to blame for it; he invented the strategy.

The genre of these second- and third-century gospels is also interesting. Many, if not most, of them imagine conversations with Jesus after his mysterious death and rising. If the earthly ministry of Mark's Jesus was shrouded in mystery, after his rising Jesus was available for quite some time to answer all the questions his disciples now have for him. Here is yet another area where learning to think like a historian and an archaeologist is so important. For the way these private conversations are reported says a great deal about how apostolic authority was believed to be established in Jesus's absence. Various possibilities suggested themselves. Proximity to Jesus and his earthly ministry was one (Peter laid claim to this, and so did Mary of Magdala—later on). Blood relation to Jesus was another (James, Judas, and Thomas all laid claim to that one, in the Gnostic gospels). Receiving a first glimpse of the risen Jesus was another source of authority (and because the accounts of this strange event differed so widely in the New Testament, everyone from Mary to Peter to John to Cleopas and his unnamed companion could claim authority in this way). Finally, the would-be apostle could establish his or her authority through rhetorical gifts of the spirit (this was largely what Paul relied upon, as he says in nearly every letter of his we possess). But these varying conceptions of early Christian authority really opened a Pandora's box; after all, every "heretic" worth his esoteric and rhetorical salt could write in a way that would establish authority, if that's all that was required to do so. Clearly, by the year 250 C.E., there were so many competing gospels, so many competing conceptions of Christian authority, all of them claiming to go back to a founding figure, that many people believed this new religion was spinning out of control. Management questions became indistinguishable from theological questions. The end result of such continuous rewriting and debate was destined to be a significantly higher Christology (an explanation of who Jesus was, specifically in relation to God) than anything available in the canonical gospels, and a church hierarchy that was structured in a decidedly top-down fashion designed to put the lid on radical Christian preaching. John's evangel had a lot to do with these changes. His was a story tailor-made for the imperial church that emerged in the fourth century.

Another way to phrase their dilemma is this: if Mark could write a gospel and imagine it as a tragedy, then why can't I write a gospel too and imagine it in a very different key? This was a major question for the first several generations of Jesus followers. As we have seen, Matthew and Luke deferred to Mark's story in general; John rejected it out of hand. The central shock lying at the heart of the Nag Hammadi discoveries is simply this: apparently, in the generations after John, scores of people in an astonishing variety of communities all felt authorized to write their own gospels. And to authorize such an author's gospel, the question of his or her authority was paramount. That, we now see, is what most of the shouting we can still vaguely hear in the New Testament was about: authority, who has it, and how we know.

Authority and Nag Hammadi

Forty years is significant for more than biblical reasons, though the Bible provides a lovely explanation of its significance: forty years is the traditional length of a human generation. Some forty years after Jesus's death, nearly all of his followers would have died as well, whether through martyrdom, accident, or old age. A second generation, no longer linked directly to Jesus and his marvelous teachings and doings, needed to articulate another way of belonging to him and to his movement: they were already beginning to imagine themselves as links in a historical chain. But the chain they were forging was one that the actual followers of Jesus in the first generation, especially Jesus's closest disciples, could not have imagined. Theirs was a different chain, binding the early followers to one another in a different way, for different reasons, in the face of new spiritual challenges and a rapidly changing Roman world. On the positive side, the next two generations of Jesus followers had the advantage of retrospect; with a larger and longer view, they could begin to reflect on what Jesus's story had meant and what it still could be made to mean in their own day.[4]

The sacred books that were discovered in those sealed ceramic jars at Nag Hammadi do not constitute a library in the traditional sense. They consist of twelve codices, all of them leather-bound and of varying quality. (The term *codex* refers to a leather-bound book with writing on both sides of each page, as opposed to a one-sided *scroll,* which had been the primary mode of producing written texts until the early Christian period.)[5] There are, in addition, eight pages that were torn out of yet another codex and inserted, unattached, into the sixth volume discovered at Nag Hammadi. What was included in this large collection of Christian curiosities was highly eclectic. The dozen books contained roughly thirty complete new manuscripts, unknown before these discoveries, as well as ten more fragmentary ones. Most of the Nag Hammadi texts are Coptic translations of what seem to have been manuscripts originally written in Greek (Coptic was the form of the Egyptian language spoken at the time but written in Greek script). There is even a fragment of a somewhat sketchy translation from Plato's Republic[6] (the influence of Greek philosophy on these various religious movements is a fascinating but vexing question). Several of the manuscripts exist in more than one version, in more than one codex, which suggests that these books were not originally part of the same "library" at all; codices like these were so expensive to produce that it would make little sense to duplicate existing manuscripts. Finally, it is noteworthy that these codices were all buried together in ceramic jars; according to the Bible itself (especially in Jeremiah 32:14–15 and 36:23), such burial is a way to preserve manuscripts for posterity. (In antiquity, you would not bury books you wanted to get rid of; you would burn or drown them instead.) I will return to the question of why these books were secreted away in an Egyptian cave later in this chapter.

Two of the most prominent words in these texts and titles are *secret* (as in "secret gospel," or "secret teaching") and *wisdom* (or *knowledge*). A number of these texts present themselves as the true way to understand certain fundamental and esoteric ideas, such as the resurrection of the dead, the origin of the material world, the nature of the soul and of the mind (which was not the same thing, for these people), and of the powers of the soul and the mind over the body. Taken together, the ascription of authorship and the subject matter of these treatises inclined scholars originally to call them "Gnostic." In fact, well before the publication of the Nag Hammadi Library, prominent New Testament scholars such as Rudolf Bultmann, Hans Jonas, and Adolf von Harnack had written superb and suggestive studies of Gnosticism.[7] The meaning and usefulness of the term has become a matter of some debate since the discoveries at Nag Hammadi.[8] The term *Gnostic* is attested in other ancient sources, especially in later antiheretical Christian writings. Thus one concern with calling these texts and their authors Gnostic is that we are actually using a pejorative term, the name their enemies chose for these religious movements. A second problem is that would-be "orthodox" Christians were every bit as interested in knowledge: *secret* knowledge they got directly from Jesus. In the forty days that separated his rising from his final ascension into heaven, Jesus was said to have revealed this *gnosis,* this esoteric knowledge as a mysterious form of spiritual truth, to his brother James, to John, and to Peter.[9] James secured it in Jerusalem, John took it to Asia Minor, and Peter brought it to Rome (where presumably he also passed it on to Mark, who then wrote it down). So this is not really a fight between know-it-all Greek philosophers and pious Christian converts. It is rather a battle between two forms of knowledge, the false and the true kind. As I showed in my summary of John's evangel, there is no arguing with rhetoric or reasoning like this. If the world really is divided between light and darkness and you claim to have the light, then all I can do is disagree or submit. That is why the arguments between these groups so quickly degenerated into name-calling: I am orthodox; you are a Gnostic, or a heretic, or something worse.

Since the name Gnostic derives from the Greek word for esoteric knowledge, there is a broader purpose to the name. Secretive and initiatory groups of various sorts were a common feature of eastern Mediterranean religious life in the Greek and Roman periods. Straddling the gap between what modern people think of as religion or philosophy and available in many flavors (there were Jewish and Christian and Zoroastrian Gnostics, after all), Gnosticism seems committed to uncovering and revealing the secret teachings that Jesus left behind for those spiritual adepts who were capable of understanding them. In this sense, Gnosticism is a catch-all category intended to cover the secret-knowledge traditions that were such a prominent feature of the spiritual counterculture in the centuries before and after Jesus's earthly ministry came to an end.

Recently, Elaine Pagels has suggested that a better way to understand this material might be to relate it to a heretical

Christian movement called Valentinianism,[10] named after the great Christian preacher Valentinus, who lived in Rome for nearly thirty years (136–165 C.E.) and then split with the church there and moved to the east and whose work was carried on by his most prominent disciples, Ptolemy and Heracleon. We know very little about the Valentinians today because their books were burned, not buried, and the only Christian records mentioning them that we had (at least, prior to 1945) were all condemnatory. We hear reports that they used dreams and ecstatic trance states and that they called themselves "spiritual Christians."[11] We know that Valentinus especially favored portions of John's evangel, and we know that Heracleon wrote a spiritual commentary on that evangel, one of the very first commentaries on a New Testament book in the history of the Christian tradition. The Valentinians read all of these texts allegorically, looking for hidden, symbolic, and esoteric meanings. And we know that one of the things that worried the people who later called themselves "orthodox" was that what people like the Valentinians did was simply too loose and uncontrollable. If the plain meaning of a text was not really plain, they reasoned, then presumably anybody could pretend to find all manner of secret sense in it.

Some of the texts buried at Nag Hammadi were clearly Valentinian in inspiration; the first one that Elaine Pagels herself translated in the early 1970s was.[12] And to be sure, some of these texts are highly imaginative—though hardly more so than the cosmic and fanciful visions we find in Ezekiel or Daniel or Revelation. In addition, there was at the time a rich tradition of allegorical reading of literary classics; the Greeks

135

and Romans had been reading Homer and Virgil and the Greek tragedians allegorically for centuries. And not much later, the North African bishop, Augustine of Hippo, would do the same thing, and quite brilliantly, with the biblical texts he knew.

There were two main problems with the Gnostic scriptures, it now appears. The first concerned the picture they painted of Jesus, of who he was and of what he accomplished. Though it is difficult to cobble together a simple portrait of Jesus from these complex texts, here is one story that many of them endeavored to tell in one way or another. It was a vaguely Platonic and deeply spiritual story, one echoed in other Christian thinkers, most notably Origen of Alexandria (c. 185–c. 254 C.E.),[13] whom we will meet again shortly. It goes something like this: God is immaterial Light, and in the beginning, all the souls that God created existed with God in that Light. One by one (Satan first), these immaterial souls fell away from that Light, took on a bodily form, and fell to earth. The only spirit who did not fall away was Jesus. He was not God, but he remained a singular and unique spirit in that he remained in complete relationship *with* God. Finally he opted, on his own initiative, to take on a body and to descend to earth anyway, in order to remind us of our true calling and our true home. Jesus thus shows the way back to God. But he is not that God. He was instead a Knowledge-Savior, not God Incarnate. Later, as we shall see, the God Incarnate party won out and declared this Knowledge-Savior to be a heretical notion.

That theological debate ran deep and it persisted. But the *real* trouble with the Valentinians and the Gnostics involved more than just their way of reading the gospels and their radically different picture of Jesus. In a word, it was their audacious claims to authority. Many of the authors of the documents uncovered at Nag Hammadi claim to be in possession of secret wisdom and secret teachings. They all claim the right to write these things down and to limit access to those whom they have deemed worthy of such secret revelation. Gnostics can have a funny way of sounding incredibly democratic and incredibly elitist almost in the same breath. But then apparently so had Jesus—according to Mark and John both.

Other Apostles, Other Gospels

Nag Hammadi was not the first place where scholars came across such strange early Christian documents, though it was far and away the greatest collection of such documents ever to be found in one place, before or since. Another codex, the so-called Berlin Codex, is a Coptic book that was discovered in the late nineteenth century in Egypt. It contains a collection of several fragmentary Christian documents that are clearly related to the ones found at Nag Hammadi. Even some of the titles correspond: the Apocryphon of John, the Wisdom of Jesus Christ, the Acts of Peter. But there is another fragment in the Berlin Codex, the first one, in fact, that is most instructive for my purposes; it is called the Gospel of Mary, and its story relates to my story in several important ways.

Though highly fragmented, the Gospel of Mary exists in three different versions, two fragmentary Greek ones and a longer Coptic section from the Berlin Codex; they are not identical.[14] The first several pages of this gospel are missing, so when we enter this story, the disciples are already doing what we see them doing in many Gnostic documents: asking for further elucidation and posing their final questions to Jesus. This became a stock scene in many of the noncanonical gospels written between 100 and 250, as I have noted: Jesus has risen up and is soon to depart forever; his followers ask for clarification on many points that were not clear when he first spoke to them; they also ask him questions that had not occurred to them before. In the Secret Book of James,[15] for instance, the story actually begins with a fascinating scene where each of the disciples is seated separately, writing down his or her own version of what had happened independent of the others, when Jesus returns to assist them and to clarify things one last time.

The disciples' questions seem every bit as philosophical as they are religious. Someone has just asked Jesus about matter, and whether it will all be destroyed in the end. Then Peter asks about sin and, by implication, about the essential goodness or badness of the world. Clearly, this has been going on for quite some time, but it is late, and Jesus must go. He urges his followers one last time to "preach the gospel of the kingdom," and cautions them against "laying down any rules beyond what I ordained."[16] Then he disappears, and the disciples are all grieved at heart. They still have questions; they still do not know enough. And they are afraid—afraid that if they do as Jesus asks, then they will be killed just as Jesus himself was.

It is Mary of Magdala who comes to the center of their circle and urges them to be of good courage. Peter responds to her plea in an especially interesting way. If he cannot ask Jesus questions anymore, then he will ask Mary. He reiterates what they all presumably already know: that Jesus "loved [Mary] more than the rest of women" and that she has had private conversations with Jesus about things "which you know but we do not nor have we heard them."[17] And right here, wouldn't you know it, just as Mary begins to reveal her secret wisdom, the manuscript breaks off again for four maddening pages. When we pick up the story, Mary has just finished, and the disciples, some of them at any rate, are outraged. Peter's brother, Andrew, refuses to believe a word of it. Anybody can say whatever they want about Jesus's private conversations, he reasons, and anyway, he cannot bring himself to believe that Jesus would choose a woman for private revelations of this kind. Peter is inclined to agree; it just seems too much. Then Levi intervenes, reminding the group that Peter "has always been hot-tempered" and too quick to change his mind. He reminds them further that even in life, Jesus "loved her devotedly,"[18] meaning perhaps "more than us." To honor Jesus and his wishes, they should listen to Mary and do what she suggests: be of good courage, preach the gospel, and not make up any new rules. Then the curtain closes.

Now at one level, this mysterious and fragmentary text is emblematically Gnostic, profoundly concerned with secret teachings, private conversations, and hidden things. But it is also a text about the complexity of authority in this new community, which is trying to figure out how to organize itself now that Jesus is gone. And it knows that the possibility of having as many gospels and teachings as there are preachers and teachers is very real. Some Valentinians were apparently not much concerned with that; the truth is manifold, they reasoned, and the whole world cannot contain it. So each person should be free to contribute his or her precious drops to the great sea of divine wisdom. Other Jesus followers were less freewheeling. Some clearly did not accept the authority of women. Some did not accept the authority of all the early followers of Jesus but relied strictly on his immediate family, his brothers and his mother. Some did not recognize the authority of anyone save Jesus himself and thus were waiting impatiently for his return. How to adjudicate such matters of fundamental importance for this community in the process of its early formation was a major preoccupation of most Jesus followers in the first two or three centuries after his crucifixion. The Nag Hammadi Library opened a window onto the full complexity of these debates, virtually for the first time.

The world that we have glimpsed through that window is in some important ways shockingly different from the one we have been taught to expect. There is conflict everywhere, disagreement about who Jesus was, what he said, what he intended, what came next. If we turn to the New Testament after reading the Nag Hammadi literature and the Berlin Codex, it is hard to miss something that literally was not easy to see before the Second World War: namely, all the conflict in the New Testament, the intense disagreements over the nature of religious authority and the nature of true Christian belief. The New Testament writers themselves do not agree on the answer to any of the questions that they pose and that the countless other noncanonical gospels help illuminate.

These early communities of Jesus followers were surprisingly contentious, experiencing great difficulty finding agreement even and especially on matters of most fundamental importance to them. The implications of that surprisingly simple fact would be difficult to overestimate. They are what constitute the real revolution in our new conception of Christian origins.

Not a Tree, an Explosion

The other great shock lying buried in the caves at Nag Hammadi is that there was no such thing as "orthodox" Christianity, not when Jesus left his disciples for the last time, and not even in the fourth century. Heterodoxy precedes orthodoxy, in any religion. After all, the concept of "orthodoxy" would not have occurred to the earliest followers of Jesus, not until some of them began to claim things about Jesus and his teachings that others found objectionable and unacceptably at odds with what they themselves believed. All that is to say that religions are not shaped like trees, with an orthodox trunk from which later heterodox (or heretical) groups splinter off in fruitless branches. Just the opposite, in fact. In the two generations following Jesus's execution, there were already any number of semi-independent Christian groups, communities that offered radically divergent interpretations of who Jesus was and what his mission meant. They all traded orally circulating sayings and miracle sources, all of which offered elusive hints at who Jesus was and what he intended. Mark wrote his tragic gospel in the first generation;

John wrote his anti-tragic evangel in the second. At the same time and thereafter, the Gnostics were doing the same things. What is clearer to us now, more than a generation after the discoveries at Nag Hammadi, is that the Christian churches did not emerge as a coherent and unified group, with a unified and coherent message, which later "heretics" then corrupted or misunderstood. Not at all. If, as Mark suggests, Jesus was dynamite, then they were dispersed from the very beginning; many different Christian communities had widely divergent views of who Jesus was, what he had accomplished, and what they should now expect. They also differed over how they understood the "scandal" of his crucifixion. Some denied it had ever happened. Some denied that Jesus had a real body, so he only seemed to die on a cross. Some said that none of this mattered anyway. Others said that it was all merely a necessary prelude to his triumphant rising and ascension into glory.

As I have suggested, a stunningly creative tragic poet whom we know as Mark landed on a remarkable way to create order out of this chaos. He cobbled together a more coherent story of who Jesus was and what Jesus intended (all the while admitting that there is much that remains mysterious about him) by weaving a number of sayings and miracles together into a uniquely Christian art form, a gospel. But that decisive decision, the invention of the most distinctive of all Christian literary genres, did not resolve the problem of competing interpretations; rather, it opened the floodgates. If Peter could refer to his private conversations with Jesus to establish his own authority, then so could Mary of Magdala. If Mark could write a gospel, then why couldn't John or Andrew or

Valentinus? The remarkable picture of Christian origins that the Nag Hammadi discoveries have helped us paint is of a world in which gospels had proliferated to such a degree that there was no longer any way to make them all cohere.

Orthodoxy came several centuries later, as a response to all this diversity. Various Christian groups, each with its own favorite gospel, or gospels, got together and tried to figure out which ones offered an acceptable portrait of Jesus and which ones did not. They were stymied for a very long time by John's evangel, precisely because it was so very different from the gospels written by Mark and Matthew and Luke, gospels that most Christian groups accepted as authoritative and Synoptic. If Mark was written around 70 C.E. and Matthew and Luke (and Acts of the Apostles) were written around 80–90 C.E., and if John was written around 90–100 C.E., then it could only be in the second and third centuries of the Christian era that we should expect to witness debates about the relationship of these four gospels to one another, as well as to all the other gospels that continued to be written and to circulate by then. That is precisely what the early Christian record indicates. But it took the discoveries at Nag Hammadi to help us see it clearly.

Scriptures to Canon

It is critically important to recall that the people we meet *in* the New Testament did not *have* a New Testament. The people we meet *in* the gospels did not *have* gospels. And if they did not have the concept of Christian orthodoxy, then they did not have the concept of a "canon" either. The Bible, for all such early Jesus followers, consisted of the roughly thirty-nine scrolls of the Hebrew Bible translated into Greek: the Torah, the Prophets, and the Writings.[19] As the Dead Sea Scrolls make clear, Jews continued to write contemporary devotional and apocalyptic literature, of course, but they did not try to include such things in their Bibles. So how did the Bible come to be imagined by followers of Jesus as containing a New Testament to accompany the Old?

The astonishing fact is that no Church council ever laid out the canonical list of acceptable Christian scriptures until after the Protestant Reformation. This was finally accomplished at the Council of Trent (1545–1563), but by then, such Vatican pronouncements were not binding on Protestants, which is why the Bibles of Roman Catholic and Eastern Orthodox and Protestant Christians are not identical.[20] The Greek word *kanon* originally meant "list," but without the normative implication of an "exclusive list," as it would later come to imply. What emerged among most (never all) Christians in the late third and early fourth centuries was simply a gradual and widespread *consensus through use,* the fact that most Christian communities read these twenty-seven books (or more, depending on how you viewed the Apocalypse of Peter,[21] the Epistle of Barnabas,[22] and the Shepherd of Hermas,[23] all enormously popular Christian writings in the second and third centuries), whichever other books they might also read devotionally.[24] That loose consensus was the basis for the formation of an ad hoc "New Testament" by the early generations of those enrolled in the Christian way. But—here is the crucial thing—they did not have a new Bible, not until much later. What they had were codices, books full of writings to which they turned for devotional inspiration. These books contained gospels, songs, poems, prayers, passages from Plato, what have you. Christians in the first several centuries thus had noncanonical codices, not Bibles in the way modern Christians have them today. The Nag Hammadi codices provide a wonderful example of precisely this sort of collection.

What we know about the first several centuries of Christian formation is tantalizing and sketchy, but certain things are clear enough. We know that these communities eventually devised a political structure of sorts,[25] with each urban community of any size led by a bishop (called an *episkopos* in Greek). These bishops played a variety of roles, but the most important thing for my purposes is that nearly all of these bishops could write and that they have left most of the record that we still possess from this period (they also seem to have been responsible for the destruction of much of the literature we no longer have). Such figures were also important political leaders, at the forefront of a curious form of spiritual counterculture, a virtual city within the city, which was apparently in the process of organizing itself throughout the urban centers of the Roman Empire. Naturally, the urgent debates about authority that we glimpse in the New Testament and in the Nag Hammadi Library persisted through the fourth century. And these authority figures became interested in defining the limits of the canon— that is, figuring out which books should be in their Christian codices, as well as in getting rid of all the other gospels they deemed "Gnostic."

For any community that accepted the Synoptic gospels and read them carefully, John's evangel presented real problems. One problem with John was that it lent itself to Valentinian spiritual and allegorical readings. As Origen, the complex third-century theologian from Alexandria, famously remarked, although John does not always tell the truth *literally,* he always tells the truth *spiritually.*[26] The important thing is not merely that John's version of Gethsemane historically contradicts the other three.[27] No, the interesting thing is Origen's distinction between "historical" and "spiritual" gospels and what that distinction allows us to trace in early Christian debates about the canon. Already by 160–170 C.E., a prominent Roman con- vert named Tatian composed a sort of "gospel harmony" that attempted to create a single, unified story of Jesus's life out of the four main accounts and attempted to show how their many apparent contradictions could be resolved. That such a work as Tatian's *Diatessaron* (literally, "through all four")[28] was under- taken at all shows how worried many Christians had become by the fact that their gospels were not really telling the same story. And the crux of their problem was John. Did Jesus's ministry last one month or three years? Did Jesus pray for a reprieve in Gethsemane or didn't he? Was Jesus human or divine or some- thing else entirely?

Since John's Jesus claimed not just to be the Son of God, but actually to be equal to God, several Christian centuries were lost in trying to figuring out exactly what that could mean and what the right way to express this divine mystery might be. If Jesus were God, then to whom was he praying in Gethsemane? The Nicene Creed, drafted in 325 C.E., explained what it meant to say that Jesus Christ was the Incarnation of God, and the Chalcedonian Creed, appended in 451 C.E. explained what it meant to imagine Jesus Christ as the "second Person" in a divine "Trinity." Athanasius (c. 296–373 C.E.), one of the more ferocious bishops in Alexandria's troubled history, stood in fervent opposition to several other popular Christian leaders who understood the Incarnation and the Trinity somewhat differently than he did. Chief among them was a bishop named Arius (c. 250–336 C.E.), also from Alexandria, who gave his name to a competing Christology known as Arian. He died unexpectedly in 336 C.E. and thus was unable to defend his views against Athanasius's continued assault. Arius clearly took the Gethsemane story more seriously than Athanasius did and found it far more problematic to harmonize with John's evangel. The critical point is that, for Athanasius as well as for other defenders of "orthodoxy," everything hinged on having the right canon and the properly episcopal conception of tradition. After being twice expelled from his city and his position and returning three times, Athanasius issued a letter in the Lenten Easter season in 367 C.E. in which he listed what he considered to be the true and traditional Christian canon.[29] His list contains all four of the gospels and, historically speaking, is the first list that is identical to the Christian New Testament today. But the bishop of Alexandria did not stop with the penning of a list. He urged all Christians in his flock to "cleanse the Church of every defilement" and then explained precisely what he meant by that: namely, the destruction of every other falsifying, Gnostic, would-be gospel.

Elaine Pagels suggests, with her wonderful flair for the dramatic and her unerring eye for the fingerprints in these historical and literary materials, that this is when the Nag Hammadi Library was hidden—for safekeeping.[30] There were a number of prestigious and surprisingly independent Christian monasteries in Egypt, one of them not far from Nag Hammadi. Nine of them (along with two nunneries) had been founded by Saint Pachomius (c. 290–356 c.e.), a noteworthy former Roman soldier who later took up baptism and the life of ascetic removal from the world. Monasticism, you see, was another important Egyptian innovation, whereby the so-called desert fathers went into individual or collective isolation and lived a life of ascetic exercise and meditation. These communities would also be the main location for Christian scribal activity and scholarship until the arrival of the printing press in Mediterranean lands. Athanasius himself had written a classic spiritual biography of Saint Antony (c. 251–356 c.e.),[31] the founding father of this ascetic desert movement, so he had great sympathy with these Egyptian monks. But the monks of Pachomius may not have sympathized with the oft-ousted bishop of Alexandria; some clearly did not. Fearing that Athanasius's intervention might result in the destruction of these important spiritual and devotional writings—records of the apostles and their beliefs, in many cases—the monks spirited them away in ceramic jars and hid them in the very caves where they would be discovered some sixteen hundred years later. And so the circle closes, with sincere questions about the canon—about marrying Mark's gospel to John's evangel—concluding with a plea for destruction and secret burial in a cave. John's vision won out in the end, all but silencing the gravelly voice and humane wisdom of Mark's gospel.

From Canon to Creeds

If the Christian churches were as besieged by murderous emperors as some third-century Christian writings would have us
believe, then it is hard to fathom how much energy these same
Christian communities expended in fighting with one another
over their canon and the creeds. Christians in the third and fourth
centuries battled over the definitions of the Incarnation and
the Trinity with the same ferocity Christians apply to abortion
or same-sex relationships these days—but then in the modern
period, "ethics" usually trumps "theology." Eusebius's *Ecclesiastical
History* spends far more time on its catalogue of heresies than it
does on the various Roman emperors and their persecutions.
He may have been trying to let Rome off the hook now that
Constantine had proved to be a friend. But whatever the reason,
in Eusebius's generation, what these Christians quarreled most
intensively about was Christology, the question of who Jesus was
and what his appearance on earth had meant. Their problem, as
should be clear by now, was how to harmonize John's portrait
of the Incarnate *Logos* with the gospel story as Mark first told
it, with its willful focus on the Gethsemane prayer and Jesus's
tragic death.

One thing seems clear enough: when Constantine the
Great (who reigned as sole emperor from 312 to 337 C.E.)
lent imperial support to the Christian churches, he expected
this somehow to contribute stability to a reign that had begun
so fractiously. Much to his surprise, Constantine found that
Christians were an uncommonly contentious lot. They could no
longer even agree about when to celebrate Easter (they still do

not; the Eastern Orthodox Christian churches celebrate it on a different liturgical calendar more closely linked to Passover than the one western Catholic and Protestant churches use).[32] This quasi-Christian emperor did something interesting about that problem, the problem of violent Christian infighting. He called an "ecumenical" council of Christian bishops (estimates at the time put their number at anywhere between 270 and 320 bishops, with an impressive accompanying entourage), modeled on the Jerusalem Council described in Acts 15:1–31. There were to be seven such ecumenical councils in all,[33] the last of which was held in Constantinople in 787, devoted to the question of the appropriate use of religious images in Christian worship.[34] In any case, Constantine commanded this first council, in Nicaea, to come to a consensus on the most divisive question of the day: Christology.

It is important for us to realize that the assembled bishops didn't spend all of their time on theology, at least not as we think of that concept today. They had been told in no uncertain terms by Constantine himself that he expected some order to be imposed on what had proved to be mostly Christian chaos until then. That required clearer political structures as well as theological clarity. Many of the minutes from these councils devote considerable time and energy to the clarification of Christian power structures and the relations between various bishops and their cities—which is to say, the appropriate lines of Christian authority. One telling conclusion the council drew was that there could never be more than one bishop in any city (presumably, this means that earlier there had been[35] and that it had created problems in the past). But what is most memorable about the Council of Nicaea is the so-called Nicene Creed, the definition of "orthodox" Christian belief about Jesus Christ as the Incarnation of God. That Creed was really aimed at a far larger and far older Christian problem: how to harmonize John's portrait of Jesus with Mark's Gethsemane prayer.

The Nicene Creed, familiar to most Christians even if they repeat it from memory and do not think about what it says, reads as follows. Try to imagine where, if anywhere, Mark's Jesus fits into this confession.

> I believe in one God: the Father, Lord of All, the maker of heaven and earth, of everything visible and invisible.
>
> And in one Lord: Jesus Christ, the Son of God; the only-begotten one; the one begotten by the Father before all ages; light from light, true God from true God; begotten not made; of the same substance with the Father, from Whom all things were made; who descended from the heavens for us human beings and for our salvation; who became flesh by the Holy Spirit and the Virgin Mary, and became human; who was crucified for us under Pontius Pilate, and suffered and was buried and rose up on the third day according to the scriptures; who ascended to the heavens and is seated at the right hand of the Father; who will come again with glory to judge the living and the dead; and whose kingdom shall have no end.
>
> And in one Holy Spirit.[36]

What is not often noticed about this Creed is that it is primarily focused on heresy, not orthodoxy. Most of these early creeds operate with the same negative logic. The whole point of the council lay in discrediting Arius and his followers, to say that the way he thought and spoke about Jesus Christ was not right. The Creed also targets a whole range of beliefs found quite clearly in the Nag Hammadi Library. The idea is that you can only get to what is right by explaining why what is wrong really is wrong. So when Christians say that they believe in one God "who created all things visible and invisible," they are insisting that they do not believe what the Gnostics believe about the creator of this material realm being a lesser and perhaps even evil deity who bore no relation to the true God. When they say that the Son was "begotten, not made," they are saying that they do not believe what the so-called Arians and Gnostics believe but rather that Christ was *not* made the way all the other creatures in creation were. He is absolutely unique, and not one among the many sons of the gods, as the pagans believed. When the Creed emphasizes the Son's "incarnate" suffering, it is once again insisting that the bishops do not believe what some Gnostics believed about the illusory quality of Jesus's embodiment; rather, for the "orthodox," Jesus's embodiment lay at the very core of their faith and was decidedly not an esoteric or spiritual illusion. In other words, the bishops are warning us what we should *not* say about Christ in order to explain what we can say and what that saying means.

As the Nag Hammadi collections make abundantly clear, *heresy came first*. Put differently, it was the very variety and dissemination of widely divergent beliefs about who Jesus was and what he said about himself that required the churches at some point to close the door on new interpretations and the circulation of new gospels. John was already pushing it, after what

Mark had done. The task of Christian theology now became in no small measure the challenge of figuring out how to keep both of these "gospels" in the same canon. The Nicene Creed attempts to explain how, yet it is difficult to escape the feeling that John's evangel won once and for all at Nicaea. It is very difficult indeed to imagine the Person described in the Nicene Creed praying as Mark imagines Jesus praying in Gethsemane. And thus, I suppose, is a religion lost as well as remade.

The bishops' solution at Nicaea also hinged on a brilliant exploitation of the subtle vocabulary that Greek philosophy made available to them. That is one reason, by the way, that when the Creed was translated into Latin, the arguments began all over again—Greek bishops felt that Latin lacked some of the philosophical subtlety and wordplay of their own more poetic language. Be sure to remember this: the doctrine of the Incarnation of God we meet in the Nicene Creed used a vocabulary that appears *nowhere* in the New Testament; this is a new and very different philosophical representation of "who he was." From now on, it will be more appropriate to refer to him as the Christ, or the Son, not as Jesus, a mysterious being who is "consubstantial" with the Father, literally "made of the same substance"—and what that means is that he is *not* "made of a similar substance," as Arius alleged.[37] These negated ideas, associated with bishops like Arius and Gnostics like Valentinus and others evident at Nag Hammadi, were declared "heretical" and "anathema." Period. There is only one bishop in a city, and urbane conversation stops when he speaks. As for all the other books and other viewpoints—they should be burned.

Anthropologists and sociologists have long been interested in the ways that human communities seem to require some real or imagined "other" against which to define themselves. Often the easiest way to tell you who I am or what I believe is first to tell you what I am *not* and what I do *not* believe. That strategy sets the limits within which I may perhaps be better able to tell you who I am and what I actually do believe. We see this logic alive and well at Nicaea, where the definition of "orthodoxy" was, as I have shown, "not heresy." There is also evidence to suggest that this same logic operated at an even more fundamental level as Christians, now free of the threat of state-sponsored persecution, turned to a fuller explanation of who they were. Their logic once again was negative and owed a great deal to John's evangel. "Christians," they began to insist, were *not* Jews and *not* Greeks. This is a shocking turnaround from the logic and the language of the rest of the New Testament, where, more often than not, *Jew* and *Greek* were neutral descriptive terms, names for groups of people who were converting to this new religious movement. And here, once again, John is the exception, the lone wolf, the sole New Testament writer who speaks with a very different voice, a voice that was deliberately trying to drown out the others.

If John's evangel was primarily responsible for the Nicene Creed, and if John's claims about Jesus's equality with God the Father made the Creed necessary, then John is also largely responsible for turning Jews and Greeks into Christianity's "others." The Christian churches would later declare war on Jews and Greeks both——all in the name of the Incarnation, and of Rome. So complete was this Johannine victory that by the eighth century, Saint John of Damascus (c. 675–749)—who was established as one of the "doctors of the Christian Church" as defined by Pope Leo XIII in 1890—went so far as to say that Judaism and Hellenism are not only heresies but actually "arch-heresies," the "mothers of all heresy," and that "out of these came all the rest."[38] The end of the matter is this: later Church traditions speak with a very different voice than Mark's tragic gospel did.

The way I phrased that last point may sound odd to North American ears. Isn't the *scripture* the heart and soul of the Christian *tradition,* after all? Yes and no, but mostly no. Because the United States of America is such a culturally Protestant country (in contrast to all of our neighbors, north and south), it is very difficult for us to imagine other ways of being Christian—Roman Catholic and Eastern Orthodox ways, for instance. This distinction is very easy for modern Christians to miss, especially if you don't know much Christian history, as most Protestants do not. Protestants tend to imagine their history in stops and starts, beginning with the idealized period of Christian origins (before Constantine) and then moving straight to the Reformation in the 1500s. Everything that happened in between—all the councils, the political organization, the novel practices and rituals—all of this is written off as the history of a mistake, a history to be avoided or ignored. The reason for this has to do with a radical new way of understanding the relation between scripture and tradition. The Nicene and Chalcedonian Creeds are a central part of the Christian tradition. Their language is not biblical and does not appear anywhere in the gospels (it comes from Greek philosophy, primarily, as I have suggested). But the Creeds are designed to instruct Christians on how to read their scriptures. Now, when you read Mark's gospel, you are meant to see that Jesus Christ is the Second Person in a Divine Trinity. Church tradition, in short, teaches you how to read the Bible.

Martin Luther eventually turned that traditional viewpoint upside down, by reimagining the relationship between tradition and scripture. Luther used the Christian *canon* to criticize and dismantle church *traditions* with which he did not agree. The Nicene Creed was one of the few traditions Luther accepted without question. But he did not accept its truth because the Roman Church taught it to him. Rather, he accepted it without question because John's evangel said so. The fact is that most scriptural religions have an implicit or explicit "canon within the canon," a sense that some Bible books are more important than others. Few Christians read the letters to Titus or Philemon with the same care they devote to the gospels. Luther, as we will see, held John's evangel in a class all by itself. We will look more closely at Luther's highly influential way of privileging John's evangel in the next chapter.

CHAPTER SIX

Martin Luther and the Beloved Disciple

How the Gospel Turned Evangelical

The Gospel is the last marvelous expression of the Greek genius, as
the Iliad is the first: . . . The stories of the Passion show that a divine
spirit, bound to the flesh, is altered by affliction, trembles before
suffering and death, feels itself in the depths of its distress to be
separated from man and God. That feeling for human misery lends
them an accent of simplicity which is the hallmark of the Greek
genius and which makes tragedy and the Iliad what they are. . . . That
accent is inseparable from the Gospel, since the feeling for human misery
is the necessary precondition of love and justice. . . . It is only possible
to love and to be just if you understand the empire of force and
know how not to respect it.

—SIMONE WEIL, "THE ILIAD, OR, THE POEM OF FORCE" (1940)

And if I cried, who in those angelic orders would listen?
Even if one of them held me close to his heart,
I would vanish in his overwhelming presence.
Because beauty is nothing more than the beginning
of a terror we can scarcely bear,
and we marvel at it because of the serene scorn
it could kill us with, and doesn't.
Every angel is terrifying.

—RAINER MARIA RILKE, "DUINO ELEGIES" (1923)

I am writing this last chapter in Atlanta, Georgia, host city of the 1996 centennial Olympic Games. When we hear the word *Olympics* today, it is difficult, if not impossible, not to think of the modern Olympics before we think of the classical Greek games—at least this was the case until the summer of 2004, when the games finally returned to Athens, Greece. Similarly, it is very hard to hear the word *Greek* as a neutral descriptive term, and to hear the word *Hellenism* as simply the name of a culture, albeit a particularly energetic and creative one, living on the far side of the age described in Chapter Five, when Christianity turned these names into heresies and terms of abuse.

The question of what to do with *Greek* once it had come to stand for *pagan heresy* preoccupied most Christians in the centuries that succeeded the emperors Constantine (r. 312–335 C.E.), who mandated tolerance for the Christian religion in 320 C.E. and Theodosius (r. 379–395 C.E.), who established Christianity as the state religion of Rome and consequently shut down all the remaining pagan sanctuaries in the empire.[1] Greek temples and sanctuaries were officially closed, not to be reopened until the nineteenth century, as excavations. The Christian polemicist Tertullian of Carthage (c. 160–235 C.E.) famously asked, "What has Athens to do with Jerusalem?"[2] and his own answer was very clear: "Nothing at all."[3] Greek theaters and oracles were condemned by important Christian writers like Tertullian, as well as bishops such as John Chrysostom of Antioch (349–c. 407 C.E.), for the ways in which they enacted "pagan" myths and violence, as well as for their idolatry.[4] Eastern Roman emperors like Justinian (r. 527–565) shut down the Neoplatonic academies in Athens in 529,[5] in large measure because they were Greek, which is to say, pagan. All of these matters—Greek myths, Greek philosophy, and Greek theater—were destined to become targets all over again in the Protestant Reformation more than one thousand years later. But why, if these things had been so long abandoned? Why make war on a Greek enemy long dead and buried?

The short answer to that question is "because of the Italian Renaissance." The term *renaissance* literally means "rebirth," and in this case, it refers to the rebirth of Christian European interest in classical Greek culture and the classical Roman world. The Greek gods and goddesses were reclaimed as subjects of creative expression in the visual arts, as the paintings of Botticelli and Raphael attest. Classical architectural models were reclaimed and put to new use in some of the most famous churches in the world, a world that consciously linked the imperial age of the Roman architect Vetruvius to that of Bramante and Brunelleschi. The recovery of classical traditions in science and medicine, sculpture and engineering, fueled many of the most momentous discoveries of "Renaissance men" like Leonardo da Vinci and Michelangelo Buonarrotti, who worked in all of these media and more. But all of this "rebirthing," all of this renewed fascination with the classical, began with the Greek language and Greek literature. Classical philology—a modern invention of the North Italian university culture sponsored by powerful patrons of leading city-states like Florence—was the engine that really drove the Italian Renaissance. And that, I believe, helps explain the complexity of what happened next.

For as many problems as the "paganness" of ancient Greece raised for some Christians, the fact remained that the New Testament was written exclusively in Greek. As I have said before, the New Testament is an important chapter in the history of Greek literature. Admittedly, the Bible had been translated into Latin by Jerome (c. 341–420 C.E.)[6] in the fourth century, in a canonical version called the Vulgate; that edition of the Bible was in use in the Roman Catholic liturgy right up until the reforms announced by the Second Vatican Council of the early to mid-1960s. I suspect that this strategic decision to translate Greek into Latin in the fifth century was also an attempt to get the Roman Christian Church away from the stigma of Greek paganism. This took place in the generation after Athanasius had clarified his own views about the canon and Christology. Even the great medieval commentator on Aristotle, Thomas Aquinas, knew no Greek; he required Latin translations of Aristotle to perform the very commentaries and theological synthesis that made him famous. Then quite suddenly, in the Renaissance, Italian and other European Christians went back to the Greek. The effects of this linguistic shift were momentous and immediate.

The most immediate effect came in the surprisingly scholarly guise of Desiderius Erasmus of Rotterdam (1466–1536),[7] arguably the most influential humanist of his age. It was Erasmus's remarkable achievement to recover the Greekness of the Christian gospels and the tragic quality of Gethsemane, which as I have tried to show, provided the gospels' original heartbeat. Erasmus did something stunning in its elegance and simplicity but revolutionary in its implications. He compared the Latin Vulgate of Jerome (a man he dearly loved and admired) to the Greek original in the New Testament. Moreover, he compared different versions of ancient manuscripts, discerning along the way how much variation there was among them. Next, he did two things with what he discovered: first, he edited a "critical edition" of the Greek New Testament, with precise attention to all of the manuscript variations; and second, he offered a new translation of the Latin Bible. The first edition of this volume sold out almost immediately in 1516. A second edition in 1519 upped the humanistic ante by making even more radical suggestions, emendations, and translational changes.[8] It is very instructive for my purposes that most of the controversy centered on what Erasmus did with John's writings.

The Renaissance Evangel

The very first line of John's evangel—"In the beginning was the *logos*"—reads as follows in the Vulgate: *In principio erat verbum,* where *verbum* clearly means "word." Erasmus offered a radical new interpretation of what he saw in this Greek text, and that complex Greek word *logos*: *In principio erat sermo,* "In the beginning was the *conversation.*" Erasmus, like most Renaissance humanists, was interested in getting a conversation started about the Bible, not in prohibiting one. For humanists such as Erasmus, paying attention to the questions posed by scripture, and all of the complexities they create, is not heresy; it is good faith. All modern scholarship, biblical and otherwise, is in their debt.[9]

The controversies intensified. There is a highly significant verse near the end of the first letter of John, which was regularly deployed in Christian debates about the Trinity. It read as follows: "There are three witnesses in heaven, the Father and the *Logos* and the Holy Spirit, and these three are one" (1 John 5:8). Erasmus discovered, much to his surprise, that none of the oldest manuscripts of the New Testament contained this verse. In fact, whenever an ancient Christian author—men such as Irenaeus, Clement, Tertullian, Origen, Athanasius, Basil the Great, Gregory Nazianzus, John Chrysostom, even Jerome and Augustine—quoted John's letter, they quoted a completely different verse. *Every one* of these prominent Christian authorities quoted a verse that reads as follows: "These three are witnesses, the spirit and the water and the blood, and these three are as one." Erasmus reasoned that later church authorities had changed the verse so as to create more "scriptural" evidence for their ideas about the Trinity. Clearly, Erasmus was already a brilliant biblical excavator, discovering human fingerprints and evidence of suspicious activity within these canonical texts.

The potentially revolutionary quality of this approach to biblical material was clear to Erasmus as well as to most of those who read and admired (or even despised) his work. But Erasmus believed himself to be working in the service of divine wisdom, *and* of the Catholic Church. His approach was radical but not revolutionary. Erasmus did not think that the implications of what he was doing would push him outside the borders of the Catholic communion. Not at all. But he had opened a door onto the individual's right to interrogate the scriptures independently and to reason to different interpretive conclusions than those currently held by Church authorities. And in doing this, Erasmus opened the floodgates of what soon became a Christian revolution: the Protestant Reformation.

The Rhetoric of Reformation

If it is still somewhat difficult for most North Americans to think in anything other than Protestant terms when they hear the word *Christian,* it is precisely because all modern people live on the far side of the Protestant Reformation. Even most Roman Catholics in North America seem to think and behave like Protestants. They can be remarkably contentious about doctrines, remarkably cavalier about Church authority and ecclesiastical traditions, and remarkably aggressive in their commitment to the right to read the Bible "on their own." That last point is the key. Until Protestants began translating the biblical texts into the languages people actually spoke and could read (few Europeans who did not work for the Church could understand Latin)—and before the invention of the printing press—very few people would ever have held a Bible in their own hands. The presence of a Bible in every home and hotel is such a commonplace in North America that we fail to realize just how novel and how radical that idea once was. Our inability or unwillingness to think historically about the emergence of Protestant Christianity in the 1500s and 1600s makes it more difficult for us to see traces of the fingerprints the Reformation has left on modern culture. In point of fact, the Reformers' reaction against the Italian Renaissance was mirrored in the twentieth century, when some Christians who began calling themselves "fundamentalists" reacted against the scholarly "higher criticism" of their Bible.

Taken together, the Constantinian Church, its checkered history of heresy hunting, its formulation of confessional creeds, and the Protestant Reformation have made it exceedingly difficult for modern Christians to recall the original Greekness of the gospel, Mark's tragic gospel in particular. Recovering the gospels' Greekness, and the tragedy of Jesus's story as Mark tells it, is the main task I have set for myself in this book. A great deal follows from that shift in attention, as we have seen. It creates the possibility of a whole new way of telling the story of Christian origins.

The shift in attention that Erasmus initiated became a revolution in the hands of Martin Luther (1483–1546), widely recognized as the premier architect of the Protestant Reformation in Europe. Luther was not a systematic theologian—his good friend Philipp Melanchthon (1497–1560) was that—but he was a brilliant sermonizer, pamphleteer, and polemicist. He was also a populist, a hard-drinking and foul-mouthed man of the people, who was also a university professor well schooled in classical languages and philosophy. Luther just so happened to be teaching in a small university town called Wittenberg, which housed one of the first printing presses in all of Saxony. And he just so happened to live at a time when all the Renaissance building programs sponsored by the Medici popes—from the Sistine Chapel to Saint Peter's Cathedral—forced the cash-strapped Vatican to find new ways to raise money. From Luther's standpoint, the Church had gotten itself into the bad business of selling salvation, and he named this offense as what it was.

There is no denying the immensity or the brilliance of Luther's achievement. The moral reforms to which he called the Church were noteworthy, and he stuck to them courageously in the face of considerable personal danger. His insistence that Christians remain focused on the central matter of their salvation and not be distracted by trifles (for so he considered most rituals and much Church tradition) also never wavered. Luther's singular powers of focus also help explain the range of his accomplishments. Adept in Hebrew, Greek, and Latin, Luther translated the entire corpus of biblical texts, both testaments, into German, and he did so with a lyricism that forever left its stamp on the German language—a stunning rhetorical achievement that even Nietzsche admired.[10] And Luther did still more. He insisted on working out the theological implications of what he was doing by putting the Bible back into people's hands. It was that tireless theological quarreling that constituted the lion's share of his labors in pamphlet after pamphlet for over thirty long years. And the best way to make sense of his enormous literary output, in essays and sermons alike, is to note that Luther—much like John and Tertullian and Athanasius and Chrysostom and countless others—fought on many fronts at once. This is one reason why John's evangel lay at the very heart of Luther's Reformation. If John wanted to supplant the Synoptic evangelists, then Luther wanted to supplant the pope and his priests.

Initially interested only in "reforming" the churches, Luther eventually declared war: on Jews, on Greeks, on the

Vatican hierarchy and most of its sacred traditions, even on the Ottoman Turks when they invaded the Balkans and laid siege to Vienna. Let me begin by pointing to several passages that demonstrate how, for Luther, John's evangel provided the rationale for everything he tried to do.

First, then, to his declaration of war on Jews. Luther's evolving anti-Semitism is legendary and assuredly represents one of the darkest chapters in this polemicist's long career. Luther argues against the Jews precisely as John's Jesus did. They possessed the scriptures that anticipated Christ's coming, they saw him face to face, and they were given the chance to believe in him. Their failure to do so invited their complete rejection and abandonment by God. If you do not see the light, then you are lost in darkness, John warned. This point is perhaps echoed most clearly in Luther's analysis of the covenant with Abraham, as described in the book of Genesis. God's promises are abundant, but they are not what contemporary Jews believed them to be, Luther warns:

> The addition of the words "I will make you exceedingly
> fruitful" and "I will make nations of you" also contradicts
> the dreams of the Jews; for the statement is explicit that the
> descendants of Abraham are to be increased, not to become
> one nation but to become many—to such an extent that many
> kings will come from him.

> But "nation" is the term applied to one definite people
> which has its own government, head, and laws. A mob of
> brigands who live without law—likewise hermits; likewise
> the Jews, who are scattered today—cannot be called a nation;

> for the Jews have been without a head or a kingdom for more than 1,500 years. They are like an army in the field without a banner and without a leader.

> Therefore the Jews have lost this promise, no matter how much they boast of their father Abraham. And not only does circumcision serve no purpose, but whatever they do in conformity with the Law is done in vain. They are no longer the people of God.[11]

No longer being *the* (singular) people of God need not be the end of the world, of course. It could mean simply that the Jews are now like everyone else, potentially saved in the new world order that Christ's coming made real. That seemed to be Luther's position in an earlier pamphlet, written in 1523, *That Jesus Christ Was Born a Jew*. Ironically, he pleaded there for greater tolerance and an end to local Jewish persecutions in German-speaking lands. As his life and thought continued to mature and to harden, however, Luther's hostility toward the Jewish people grew fiercer. Jews become, in Luther's later years, symbolic of everyone who had ever been given the chance to accept the evangel and then rejected it. This is precisely how John saw the Jews, we will recall, most notably in the ninth chapter of his evangel, when followers of Jesus are expelled from the synagogues. Luther's rhetoric of damnation intensifies until it becomes almost hard to hear.

His infamous essay *On the Jews and Their Lies* makes this brutally apparent.[12] Its political recommendations are shocking, especially in the post-Holocaust world: synagogues should be burned, Jewish houses should be razed, their holy books should be confiscated, and finally, Jews should be expelled from the country, this last proposed, ironically, as an imitation of God's (read: the Romans') expulsion of them from Israel after the Second Jewish Revolt in the year 135 C.E. This is all rather astonishing, and so far from his pleas for tolerance two decades earlier that one cannot help wondering what happened.

Luther claims that he is responding to an unknown Jewish pamphlet; he seems to believe that it insulted Jesus and Mary by suggesting that the story of the Virgin Birth (a story that is not told in Mark or John, be sure to note) was actually designed to cover up Jesus's illegitimacy. But Luther was a lifelong polemicist who gave as good as he got; name-calling would not have pushed him to this extreme all by itself. A likelier possibility is that Luther had hoped that many Jews would convert to his version of the evangel if given more time. This essay is born of his frustration at their failure to be moved. Here is where the influence of John's evangel on Luther's polemics becomes clearer. Light and dark are two extremes that never meet. The good news is only good news for a short time; it demands a choice. Failure to accept it is disastrous, and disaster lasts forever.

> Do not engage much in debate with Jews about the articles of our faith. From their youth they have been so nurtured with such venom and rancor against our Lord that there is no hope until they reach the point where their misery finally makes them pliable and they are forced to confess that the Messiah has come, and that he is our Jesus. Until such a time it is much too early, yes, it is useless to argue with them about how God is triune, how he became man, and how Mary is the mother

of God. No human reason nor any human heart will ever grant these things, much less the embittered, venomous, blind heart of the Jews. As has already been said, what God cannot reform with such cruel blows, we will be unable to change with words and works. Moses was unable to reform the Pharaoh by means of plagues, miracles, pleas, or threats; he had to let him drown in the sea.[13]

That last line is the really ominous one. Luther knows well that, according to a number of repeated passages in Exodus, it was God who hardened Pharaoh's heart,[14] a point that raises large and troubling questions about God's justice, and should cause us to remember that Gethsemane and the Passion of Christ took place during Passover, a festival that commemorates precisely this act of retributive divine justice. Luther's conclusion is thus even more distressing than the obvious plea for killing in the name of Christ. He seems actually to be arguing that God's plan has been to condemn and blight and eliminate the Jews all along. If there be stench and muck here—recurrent terms of abuse in Luther's prose—then it is muck of Luther's own making.

Turning from such polemics to more positive doctrines, we come to Luther's related polemics against the Greeks. The pithiest idea lying at the heart of the Protestant Reformation is neatly encapsulated in one phrase: *sola scriptura, sola fides,* "scripture alone, and faith alone." What Luther intended by this pithy pronouncement is quite clear. Scriptures and faith alone can ensure Christian salvation. Not "reason," and not "works" (and probably not "tradition"). Luther cuts through the knotted mess of ever more complicated Church traditions with the sword of his Bible. Any Church tradition, he reasons, that does not accord with the Bible is to be rejected or ignored. What is fascinating is how often Luther's condemnation of the Greeks emerges precisely here, when he confronts Church traditions with scripture—which seems logical enough in the Renaissance, when classical learning was itself being sponsored by the Church. "Scriptures alone" is Luther's antidote to the Christo-pagan corrosive of scholarly work like Erasmus's.

> This is sufficient indication that we should not look to the works and teachings, the glosses and lives of men, but rather fix our eyes on the pure Scriptures and retain what is best from the lives and teachings of all the saints, so that we may not undertake to snatch up everything they do and say, but judge all things carefully and choose with discrimination what is born of the Scriptures. . . .

> However, they think, and everyone believes, that they fare well if they rely on these three things, the teachings of men, the examples of the saints, and the glosses of the fathers. In this no one may doubt or oppose them. They rule with self-assurance and imagine that they alone possess the Holy Scriptures which they have excellently and well caught up in these three vessels. Besides all this, they have fallen even deeper into the abyss of darkness, because they claim that natural insight and pagan knowledge are also a good means to discover truth. Our universities have boundlessly erred in claiming this position when they teach that no one may be a theologian without Aristotle, the best of Christians! O blindness beyond all blindness! We could of course tolerate it, if they mean by natural knowledge that fire is hot, three and five are eight, and so on, all of which

are well known to natural reason. But they outdo themselves and dream idle dreams and useless thoughts about things which do not exist, and about which they are ignorant. It is distressing to think of their mad and senseless zeal for study and the cost and trouble they expend on it, so that the evil spirit simply laughs at them. God plagues them as they have deserved, because they do not cling to the pure Scriptures. Consequently they are all condemned to devour such muck and stench of hell, and to perish.[15]

What is most instructive here is not the barb against teaching Aristotle and Greek philosophy among Christians, nor is it the assault on "natural reason." (Luther quipped that he took up his professorship in theology at Wittenberg just so that he could dodge the responsibility of teaching Aristotle's *Nicomachean Ethics,* and stick to the scriptures instead.) No, the real punch of passages like this one lies in the conclusion of damnation, its polemical emphasis on the muck and stench of hell. That rhetorical bombast inspired very real violence among his followers, almost immediately.

"Faith alone" was Luther's succinct recapitulation of the heart of Paul's gospel message, the idea that Jews were condemned under the Law of Moses because of the "original sin" of Adam, which rendered them incapable of keeping to a legal code that was clear and simple and, as Moses emphasized, possible (Deuteronomy 29:29). Original sin made it impossible, said Paul, and in a brilliant additional move, he reasoned that the whole purpose of the Mosaic Law lay in making us see that we can do nothing worthwhile on our own, that "good works" cannot bring us closer to God. Now, it is one for thing for Paul, who never had access to any text from the New Testament, to say such a thing. But it is quite another for Luther, who not only knew the entire New Testament but spent years translating it, to say what Paul said. The problem is that there are so many other passages in the New Testament—portions of John's first letter, as well as the letters of James and of Peter—that speak of "good works" most appreciatively. There is, in addition, the Sermon on the Mount, where Jesus enjoins his listeners "to be perfect, as your Father in heaven is perfect" (Matthew 5:48). Luther cuts through this confusion in Christian ethics, the confusing link between salvation and sanctification, in a fascinating way, and this time his sword has a name: it is John.

> The statement "that they may see your good works and give glory to your Father who is in heaven" is in accordance with St. Matthew's way of speaking; he usually talks this way about works. Neither in his Gospel nor in those of the other two evangelists, Mark and Luke, do we find such a great emphasis upon the profound doctrine of Christ as we do in St. John and St. Paul; instead, we find them talking and exhorting about good works. Of course, it is appropriate that in Christendom both should be preached, yet each in keeping with its nature and value. First and highest is the proclamation about faith and Christ, then comes the emphasis upon works. The evangelist John discussed the chief article thoroughly and powerfully, and hence he is regarded as the highest and foremost evangelist.[16]

Here we see the main line of argument that Luther uses repeatedly to make some of his most important and innovative theological points. John's evangel (perhaps along with Paul's Letter to the Romans) is the single most important book in the entire

Bible. John is the "canon within the Christian canon," and the entire Bible should be read through the interpretive lens of John's presentation, John's understanding of who Jesus was and what his coming meant. Luther says this most explicitly in the preface to his translation of the New Testament. It is worth remarking that most translators write prefaces to their translations in which they try to explain what motivated the interpretative choices they have made. Erasmus did this. Luther did it, too,[17] and his preface really seals the deal:

> If I had to do without one or the other—either the works or the preaching of Christ—I would rather do without the works than without the preaching. For the works do not help me, but his words give life, as he himself says (John 6:63). Now John writes very little about the works of Christ, but very much about his preaching, while the other evangelists write much about his works and little about his preaching. Therefore John's gospel is the one, fine, true, and chief gospel, and is far, far to be preferred to the other three and placed high above them. So, too, the epistles of St. Paul and St. Peter far surpass the other three gospels, Matthew, Mark, and Luke.[18]

Luther's demotion of the Synoptic gospels is striking, to say the least. And his reasons are not hard to find. The fundamental theological revolution Luther unleashed was inspired by his complete agreement with John's far more elevated Christology. The point to emphasize is Jesus's divinity in the face of human fallenness. Only John's evangel makes that connection plain.

> We should remember this passage and similar passages to strengthen our faith in the true divinity and humanity of

Christ. . . . Therefore the evangelist John is master above all
other evangelists, for he treats of this doctrine of Christ's divinity and humanity persistently and diligently. He joins these two
natures together. When Christ becomes man, He speaks
to us, performs miracles, and dies according to His humanity.
And then His divinity is also established with plain words.[19]

Plain words. Luther's reasoning is plain as well: Gethsemane
admits a level not just of humanity but of actual doubt, and
that Luther finds completely unacceptable in the Savior of
humankind. Faith stands alone, and all it requires is an act
of will that denies anything that runs counter to what you
wish to believe. (Luther engaged in a very public quarrel with
Erasmus in 1524 and 1525 on these very points.) Such an abso-
lutizing view of the world will almost inevitably result in some
pretty severe line-drawing. Many people—Jews, Greeks, even
Roman Catholics—will eventually be excluded by such reasoning. And in a way that seems quite new in modern Christian
rhetoric, Luther's Protestant polemics replace the language of
forgiveness with that of judgment, damnation, and the stench
of hell. John's evangel is now to be used as a weapon in the
fight against Mark's more tragic, and more humane, version of
Jesus's doubt and demise.

Evangelical Exercises in Killing Compassion

There is a famous story that is often invoked as marking the
beginning of the Protestant Reformation. In the autumn of
1517, Martin Luther, then still an Augustinian monk, allegedly

attached a list of ninety-five theses to the door of the Castle Church in Wittenberg (he explicitly mentioned the outrageous expense of the new Roman basilica of Saint Peter in three of them), and the storm of Christian controversy broke. There is no question that this, the first of Luther's many theological pamphlets, received immediate attention and inspired immediate, even violent, Church reactions in some quarters. But in fact, Luther may have nailed the theses to a doorway in the neighboring town of Mainz, or he may have posted them in both places at the same time. In any case, his father confessor, Vicar General Johannes von Staupitz, who was sympathetic to Luther's criticisms, was also entirely convinced of this monk's spiritual sincerity. He would later release Luther from his vows of obedience, precisely so that he could engage in public debate with his superiors. Other local Church officials, prominent bishops named Tetzel and Albrecht, were not so sanguine. Pope Leo X was in no mood for such disputations either; he had wars to wage and basilicas to build. But disputes there were, and when a famous local debater, Johannes Eck of Ingolstadt, got word of Luther's views, he coined a new name for anyone who supported him. He called them "Lutherans"; the name was a sneer intended to dismiss the whole thing as the suspect opinions of one rabble-rousing monk. Today, of course, Lutheran is the perfectly respectable name of a Protestant denomination. But in the beginning, Luther didn't like the name any more than Eck did.

In response, Luther coined a name of his own (he also coined a name for Eck and his other critics: "Mainz whoremongers and fat paunches"). Luther did not call himself a

Protestant, since "protest" didn't really capture the essence of what he was up to. And he did not call himself a reformer, at least not yet, though he would probably have preferred that term to revolutionary, since he did not yet imagine breaking with the Roman Church any more than Erasmus did. The name Luther coined for his movement was *evangelical,* and that name took hold among many of his followers. The name comes from the Greek word for the gospel, *evangelion,* and it was designed to highlight the "good news of God," the very thing that Luther argued had been corrupted by the Roman Church to such a degree that Christians were in danger of losing it. What I like about the name is the way it highlights the connection between Luther's evangelical fervor and John's evangel. The name stuck. It is still in use today.

But the sneer in Eck's name stuck too and posed a problem that Luther and his followers could never entirely resolve. How could they be sure that they were right? Who were they to buck a millennium and a half of evolving Church traditions in the name of their own private reading of the scriptures? "How do you know? How do you know?" This is the haunting question that started Luther on his intensely personal religious quest, decades earlier. It is another one of the most famous stories Luther told, in a sermon penned some thirty years after the event it describes. In 1510, Staupitz sent the promising young monk to Rome to mediate a dispute between quarreling factions of Augustinians. Luther crossed the Alps on foot, arrived in the imperial city, and stayed for a month. He was unimpressed by the classical ruins, though there is some evidence that he sniffed around more than he needed to. At the end of his stay, Luther made the obligatory climb up the Santa Scala at the Lateran Palace in Rome, stairs believed to be the same ones that Christ climbed into the court of Pontius Pilate, stairs that were later removed to Rome by Constantine's mother, Saint Helena.[20] As Luther ascended the stairs, a question started nagging at him, a question about tradition, a question that would never leave him and never gave him rest: "Who knows whether this is really true?" That question—and Luther's desperate, lifelong quest for certainty—provided the panicked impulse to his "evangelical" Reformation.

Luther's questioning of authority was of a piece with his questions about knowledge. The poignancy in so many of Luther's writings is the prominent place that doubt occupies in it and how honestly he confronts it. The darker side of Luther's Christian Renaissance (it was also conceived as a "rebirth," not of classical wisdom this time, but of primitive Christian faith) lay in the way Luther rebelled against his own doubt, and others', in such violent terms. Sensitive to the power of the Gethsemane story, Luther turned away from it, and gave himself to John instead.

Sola scriptura, sola fides. Luther's anxiety is neatly couched in this phrase as well. Scripture, *not* reason; faith, *not* works. Luther's lifelong anxiety lay in the fact that *doing* good cannot help you know if you *are* good. Ultimately, we must confront the fact that no one is good except God and then fall on God's mercy. But this idea only intensified Luther's problem, because you cannot know either one. Faith is not knowledge, so you can only try to live *in* it, as steadfastly as you may. And the idea of *original* sin complicates matters still further: How can you ever know if you have really been steadfast enough, especially in a fallen world of flux and change? If you think that you have been faithful, then most likely you're not. These questions haunt Luther's later life and work, and one senses that the violence of his rhetoric was as often as not a reaction against his own lingering doubts.

That is why the name he chose for the movement, "evangelical," is so important for my purposes in this book. In the face of doubt and against false "traditional" authority, Luther invokes the gospel. But which "gospel"? Mark's or John's? Luther's answer is absolute: John's and only John's evangel can bring you the certainty you need. Luther found in John's portrait of Jesus a surety and a confidence that he found nowhere else. In this way, Luther's "evangelicals" gradually lost sight of the alternative genius of Mark's gospel, the quieter conviction that does not shout on its own behalf, and the more muted hope that in this topsy-turvy and God-haunted world, God can turn doubt itself into gospel. That is the redemptive tragedy that Mark imagined unfolding in Gethsemane, and that is precisely the compassionate Christian vision that John's evangel repudiated. Communities that choose John exclusively over Mark fall into this same temptation, the temptation to lose any sense of tragedy, any sense of original Christian compassion, preferring the rhetoric of muck and stench and damnation instead.

Evangelism in America

The relevance of these final matters to the complex and increasingly polemical contemporary religious landscape in North America cannot be overestimated. The impact of the

Protestant Reformation on the unfolding of North American culture even in the colonial period is well known. The United States is a very Protestant country, culturally speaking. We still have Protestant communities today that call themselves "evangelical," though the term *fundamentalist* has become more public and more prominent in recent decades. It is important to note, however, that these two rather different Christian groups are not identical in their theology or in their politics.[21] It is also important to realize that "fundamentalism" is really possible only among Protestants; it would make little sense for a Roman Catholic to be a "fundamentalist," since Catholics do not believe in turning to "scripture alone." Still, contemporary fundamentalists and evangelicals know their history well enough, though they usually know their Bible a lot more selectively, and they combine these two forms of knowledge to paint a portrait of Jesus Christ as the original religious nonconformist. Luther was another in that proud line of Christian prophets, they argue, so much so that fundamentalists can claim that the "ultimate religious nonconformity came with the Protestant Reformation" (why, I wonder, not with Mark's gospel?). Such fundamentalists even admire the Renaissance humanism of men like Erasmus, men who opened the doors to the possibility that Christians "could once again read the Bible in its original languages and find therein the true Church of the New Testament era."[22]

What Christian fundamentalists such as the late Jerry Falwell do not address in so saying are the two points that serve as the very foundation for this book: (1) the "New Testament era" was one of bitter contestation and conflict over Jesus's nature and authority, as well as over the authority structure of early Christian leadership (the Nag Hammadi Library makes this very clear); and (2) Erasmus's scholarship made any claims to "biblical inerrancy" very difficult to comprehend, precisely by pointing out to us that there never was one version, nor one "original" ancient manuscript, of the biblical texts. Thus the existence of noncanonical gospels is not the only challenge for Christian authority these days. The deep disagreements within the gospels themselves, as well as the later addition of scenes and stories that do not square with the originals, make the work of discerning early Christian meaning very difficult indeed. The questions I have underlined in this book are not small matters, like questions about discrepant historical chronologies, but rather matters of the greatest urgency for anyone interested in professing the Christian faith with clarity and care. Did Jesus pray in despair in Gethsemane, or did he refuse that prayer? Did Mark's gospel conclude without a resurrection appearance, or did Mark's Jesus make a promise that his followers could drink poison without fearing the consequences? Did John's first letter refer to the Trinity, or to baptism and the Eucharist? In a world where scriptural monotheists must coexist with other people representing other faith traditions, what is the appropriate place of conversion, or condemnation, or damnation? If the gospel were conceived as a Christian tragedy, how might this help us reconceive proper Christian compassion?

As I have suggested, one of the most interesting, albeit subtle, aspects of John's evangel is that it explicitly intends to *replace* the Synoptic gospels. Luther understood that very well, and he granted John's evangel the very supremacy that it claimed for itself. But the only way John could sell his version of the gospel message was to take it to new places, to audiences that had not heard the story—Mark's story—before. John's evangel, alone of the four, is "evangelical" in this sense too, written for people who do not know Jesus's story yet. Mark's gospel was written by a Christian for a Christian audience in the hopes that by telling an old story in a new way, new truths could be revealed and the twin dangers of arrogance and lack of compassion could be exposed as the greatest threat to genuine Christian communion. John's evangel clearly admits as much: "Now Jesus did many other signs in the presence of the disciples, which are not written in this book; but these are written that you may believe that Jesus is the Christ, the Son of God, and that believing you may have life in his name" (John 20:30–31). Presumably, the things written in Mark's book are such things, things John's evangel was designed to supplant or replace. This logic helps explain one of the most peculiar gestures to which many contemporary Christian communities put their energy: the "conversion" of people, Roman Catholics and Eastern Orthodox primarily, who are already Christian. The reasoning is plain enough, and it has a very long pedigree that takes us all the way back to Nag Hammadi: such people think that they are Christians, but they are the wrong kind, which is as much as to say that they are not really Christians at all.

The link between Luther's Reformation and the current religious landscape in the United States is a deeply ambivalent one. Certainly the close attention to biblical texts, the desire to "get them right," is a laudable development. So too, a healthy suspicion of authority, one that does not degenerate into anarchism or name-calling, is a salutary and eminently democratic thing. But there is a darker side to every Renaissance, and that is as true of Luther's as of any other. That dark side has been increasingly visible in the past thirty years in the United States. The current fundamentalist landscape in the nation is too often characterized by Luther's strategy of theology through polemic. Name-calling takes the place of theology and careful thinking about matters worth getting right. Perhaps this has always been the case; we saw ample evidence of the same strategy in John's evangel and in the early churches. Self-definition often comes at the expense of and condemnation of "others," of those whom we are not. This strategy is almost always intensified in an age when Christians believe the end of the world is at hand. Luther clearly believed this later in his life, so that by the time he concluded that the anti-Christ (not the pope) was actually seated on the throne of Saint Peter, and while the armies of the Ottoman Empire were camped outside the gates of Vienna, he felt sure that there was very little time left. Such an apocalyptic belief can create a very impatient theology, one that more easily justifies getting rid of Jews and Greeks and Muslims and Catholics and whomever else you care to name. Scrolling through the books and Web sites, the countless postings and pronouncements of evangelicals and fundamentalists in the current cultural climate make this same strategy abundantly clear. Praying for your enemies is a forgotten Synoptic art, drowned out by the ferocity of John's judgments.

Clearly, there are reasons for what such groups believe; people are rarely dupes or fools. But people—and Luther more than most—can be highly selective in their reading and very impatient with a world (and a Word) they do not control. It seems clear to me that this is why the same Mark who imagines Gethsemane as he does reminds us of Jesus's warning against predicting the time for the end of the world. I fail to see how the current political agenda of Christian fundamentalists in the United States of America can be made compatible with the multiethnic and multireligious society this same nation now takes nearly for granted and embraces as essential to its social mission. I fail to see how the desire to convert this same nation to Christ can avoid the violence, both rhetorical and real, that Luther's polemics produced. In this sense, these groups are literally and figuratively playing with fire.

The selective reading of the New Testament is virtually a requirement in order to make this "evangelical" political strategy successful. If you read John's evangel, and only John's evangel, then you will never get to Gethsemane, never get to the compassionate heart of the earliest Christian gospel, Mark's gospel, the one whose tragic vision is well worth rehabilitating today. But if you read John, and only John, then all the rest may follow.

After the final no there comes a yes
And on that yes the future world depends.
No was night. Yes is this present sun.
If the rejected things, the things denied,
Slid over the western cataract, yet one,
Only one, one thing that was firm, even
No greater than a cricket's horn, no more
Than a thought rehearsed all day, a speech
Of that self that must sustain itself on speech,
One thing remaining, infallible, would be
Enough. . . .
Out of a thing believed, a thing affirmed:
The form on the pillow humming while one sleeps,
The aureole above the humming house. . . .

It can never be satisfied, the mind, never.

—WALLACE STEVENS, "THE WELL DRESSED MAN WITH A BEARD"

The story I have tried to tell in this book is relatively simple, though its implications (like the details) are not. Within two generations of Jesus's final departure, two roads diverged on the Christian way. A single generation after Jesus's scandalous crucifixion, Mark chose to weave together various oral traditions about Jesus into a marvelously supple literary tapestry he called a "gospel." He modeled this gospel on Greek tragedy, and he understood the anguished prayer in Gethsemane to be its tragic heartbeat. One generation after Mark, a very different kind of Christian wrote a very different kind of story, one designed to replace Mark's version, not to supplement or enhance it. The crux of what John did to Mark's tragic gospel (and to the other Synoptic versions as well) was to deny that Jesus ever prayed this way, in a garden or anywhere else. John's Jesus lacks all doubt and all fear, and for this very reason, he is terrifying to those around him. He simply is not human. And this inhumanity creates a very harsh and inhumane version of Mark's story. I have suggested that John's story is not a gospel at all, by Mark's standards. The emotional responses of pity and compassion simply don't work for John; fear and judgment are the primary emotional responses in John's evangel.

Two roads diverged on the Christian way in the early second century, and while a great many Christian bishops and commentators and councils all tried to keep the two together, John's version in some ways had to win out, had to silence large portions of Mark's tragic gospel and Jesus's Gethsemane prayer. For if you take John at his word, then this is a battle between good and evil, between light and darkness, and compromises do not work in such a world. There are winners and losers, and John aims to win. Subsequent Christian history demonstrates the extent of John's victory, and the cost of that victory, given how little attention most Christians pay to Mark's quieter, more chastened, and more cautious gospel.

John, I have suggested, wrote an evangel, not a gospel, and it has served the evangelical purposes of Christians very well.

John's evangel was the book of choice for Martin Luther, as it is for most evangelicals and fundamentalists still today. I gestured briefly to the contemporary setting in the final pages of Chapter Six and would like to pick up on that point here at the end.

One of the most striking features of the self-proclaimed "religious right" in the United States is how much its rhetorical strategies owe to John's evangel. The most political portions of the fundamentalist movement in this country also fight on many fronts, fronts they somewhat oddly conceive as linked in a single, global war. They defend a literalist view of the Bible against most critical scholarship, be it historical or archaeological or both. They defend a creationist view of the world's history against the entirety of modern evolutionary and geological and astronomical science. They defend a very particular Victorian sexual and marital morality against every other kind. And they link their religiosity to a surprisingly unreflective version of patriotism and a belief in the foreordained role of the United States in the contemporary world as that world comes to its inevitable close. They defend all of this despite the fact that Jesus said not one word about any of these issues (excepting a few surprisingly lax comments on sex and marriage, and one rather harsh one) and despite the fact that the existence of the western hemisphere is never imagined in any biblical text.

John might have argued this way, and did so. Mark never would. One of the crucial aspects of Mark's tragic gospel that is surprisingly easy to miss are his repeated pleas for caution, for muting our certainty, for avoiding the hubris of saying that what was difficult for Jesus will somehow be easier for us.

According to Mark, no one fully understood Jesus, not even when he was here. The clearest statements he made were misunderstood or misrepresented by his own disciples because they did not want a tragedy. Hypocrisy is everywhere, so Mark's Jesus cautions his friends to be careful and to be watchful—of religious leaders and political leaders, alike. The world is an uncertain place, and the future is known only to God. The first will be last. All we can do faithfully is to watch, to listen, to pay closer attention, and to cultivate our compassion.

This book was born of that same tragic call and those same patient habits. It owes its conception to Mark's tragic gospel, to a former professor of mine to whom it is dedicated, and to the eloquent thumbprint of a pirate whose name I will never know.

NOTES

Introduction

1. Clark Butler (ed.), *Hegel: The Letters* (Bloomington: Indiana University Press, 1984), p. 57.

Chapter One

1. For more on the relationship between storytelling and the formation of religious tradition, see my essay "The Whole Story" (forthcoming). For more on the gospels, see my *Tragic Posture and Tragic Vision: Against the Modern Failure of Nerve* (New York: Continuum, 1994), pp. 181–193. Note that this way of thinking about preaching and the gospels has inspired a movement in the past twenty years called "narrative theology." A good introduction is Stanley Hauerwas and L. Gregory Jones (eds.), *Why Narrative? Readings in Narrative Theology* (Grand Rapids, Mich.: Eerdmans, 1989).

2. In John 19:25, one of the Marys who appears at the empty tomb is referred to as "the wife of Clopas," suggesting perhaps that this is the same man who was thus widely associated, albeit indirectly, with the original report of the rising of Jesus. Later Church traditions claimed that he was the brother of Joseph and that his son, Simeon, was Jesus's first cousin. Simeon was officially remembered as the second bishop of Jerusalem, taking over after Jesus's brother, James. Clearly, in the capital city of Jerusalem at least, Jesus's family ran the show. See Eusebius's *Ecclesiastical History* III.1.22 and IV.5. For the Greek text of Eusebius's *History,* I am using the Loeb Classical Library edition in two volumes, translated by Kirsopp Lake (Cambridge, Mass.: Harvard University Press, 2001; originally published 1926).

3. Luke 24:13, though some manuscript versions triple that distance, most notably the oldest manuscript copy of the entire New Testament, the famous fourth-century *Codex Sinaiticus.*

4. She is identified as "the mother of James," but since James was Jesus's brother (Mark 6:3; Matthew 13:55), this would logically follow—unless the James in question was another man, the so-called son of Zebedee (Mark 3:17; Matthew 10:2). I'll return to this confusion over names shortly.

5. The Greek word Luke uses is *pneuma,* the same word used by certain Gnostic groups to describe their movement as "spiritual" (literally, "pneumatic") Christianity.

6. We might guess that this is a reference to the wounds inflicted in his crucifixion and the memorable story in which one disciple, Thomas, refuses to believe that this is Jesus until he touches the wounds himself. But this figure of "doubting Thomas" comes from John, not Luke. For a marvelous survey of the cultural reception of this image in literature and painting, see Glenn W. Most, *Doubting Thomas* (Cambridge, Mass.: Harvard University Press, 2005).

7. *Preaching* (in Greek, *keryssein* is the verb and *kerygma* is the noun) seems to have been a technical term used by these early followers of Jesus to mean telling a story as Jesus did on the Emmaeus road, a story that begins with Moses and runs right through the prophets—that is to say, a story that takes the listener from the covenant with Abraham up to the present day (see Acts 7:1–53).

8. It is one of the strangest and most striking features of the Christian climate in North America today that most Christians find the idea that Jesus had brothers and sisters more shocking than the fact that he was executed like a common criminal. Both Mark (6:3) and Matthew (13:55) clearly mention four brothers by name: James, Joses (or Joseph), Judas, and Simon. This raises an obvious question: Were Jesus's brothers disciples? Later traditions (recorded in the gospels of Thomas and Judas) suggest that Judas was not only a brother but actually Jesus's twin. The confusion has to do with the common Mediterranean practice of naming an eldest son after a

paternal grandfather. At Phalasarna on Crete, for instance, among our roughly forty workmen, we had four men named Yiannis, three named Nikos, and three named Manolis. According to Mark (3:13–19), among Jesus's twelve disciples, there were two named Simon and two named James, and according to Luke (6:12–16), two named Judas as well.

9. The classic presentation of this idea is William Wrede, *The Messianic Secret in the Gospel,* trans. J.C.G. Grieg (Greenwood, S.C.: Attic Press, 1971; originally published 1901).

10. For more on the creation of this significant Greek translation in the Egyptian city of Alexandria, see Abraham Wasserstein and David J. Wasserstein, *The Legend of the Septuagint: From Classical Antiquity to Today* (New York: Cambridge University Press, 2006).

11. 1 Corinthians 1:23. This is often translated as "stumbling block," though the Greek word is very clear: *skandalon.*

Chapter Two

1. Compare the story set in Bethlehem in Luke (2:1–40) to the emphasis on the family's flight to Egypt and relocation to Nazareth in Matthew (2:1–23). The question of where Jesus was originally from is given a prophetic interpretation at John 4:19–26. Mark says hardly a word about this.

2. This point is made wonderfully by Vernon K. Robbins in *Jesus the Teacher: A Socio-Rhetorical Interpretation of Mark's Gospel,* rev. ed. (Minneapolis, Minn.: Augsburg Fortress, 1992).

3. But no wise men from the east; that is Matthew's story (Matthew 2:1–12).

4. Jeffrey Stout, *Democracy and Tradition* (Princeton, N.J.: Princeton University Press, 2004), p. 226, quoting Edward Albee's *Zoo Story.*

5. Many of the oldest manuscripts of the canonical gospels, but not all of them, contain these two bracketed verses. The most significant is the earliest complete collection of the gospels we possess, the fourth-century *Codex Sinaiticus,* now housed in London. Virtually

every major Christian writer from the second through the fifth centuries (among them Justin Martyr, Irenaeus, Epiphanius, Eusebius of Caesarea, John Chrysostom, Jerome, and Augustine) knows these verses and quotes them. I've already mentioned Eusebius; the rest will make their appearance later on.

6.   The first half of Luke's story about Gethsemane really puts the premium on prayer. When he first enters "the place," Jesus tells his disciples to pray (Luke 22:40). Next, he goes off alone, about a stone's throw, and prays (22:41). In the company of an angel from heaven, his agony intensifies in prayer (22:44). After sweating drops of blood, Jesus rises from prayer (22:45) and returns to his disciples, only to find them asleep. So he repeats his prior warning now as a stern command: pray (22:46). Prayer makes all the difference, in Luke's opinion. And as we will see, through prayer, Jesus is now ready for what will happen next, as his friends are not.

7.   See the entry on *peira* in Gerhard Kittel, *Theological Dictionary of the New Testament,* Vol. 6, trans. Geoffrey W. Bromiley (Grand Rapids, Mich.: Eerdmans, 1964–1976), pp. 23–36.

8.   *Theological Dictionary of the New Testament,* Vol. 6, p. 24.

9.   This may reflect the influence of Paul; see, for instance, Acts 3:18, 4:28, and 13:48.

10. *Iliad* 7:282, 293.

11. By contrast, in the gospels of both Mark (15:34) and Matthew (27:46), Jesus's last word is a shattering cry of despair: "Why?"

12. The phrase "your will be done" also appears in what has come to be known as the Lord's Prayer, but only in Matthew's version; it is absent from Luke's. See Matthew 6:10.

13. Frank Kermode reads it this way in his marvelous book *The Genesis of Secrecy* (Cambridge, Mass.: Harvard University Press, 1979), and on this basis, he develops a reading of Mark's gospel that draws out all of its most essential paradoxes (see esp. pp. 141–145).

14. For more on this strange form of address, see Joseph A. Grassi, "Abba, Father (Mark 14:36): Another Approach," *Journal of the American Academy of Religion,* 1982, *50,* 449–458.

15. As I explain in Chapter Five, Christians expended tremendous energy over the next four centuries trying to hammer out the theological implications of the claim that Jesus had a real human body, on the one hand, and a will of his own, on the other. He couldn't simply be God—Gethsemane is the story that proves that—and that's the main reason why John denied it ever happened.

16. "The 'danger' of Mark's approach to prayer is not that it will be taken too seriously but that the formative document of the community that experienced both divine power and devastating persecution will be trivialized by a church that experiences neither." Sharon Echols Dowd; "'Whatever You Ask in Prayer Believe' (Mark 11:22–25): The Theological Problem of Prayer and the Problem of Theodicy in Mark," dissertation, Emory University (1986). This work is also available as *Prayer, Power, and the Problem of Suffering: Mark 11:22–25 in the Context of Markan Theology* (Atlanta: Society of Biblical Literature, 1988).

17. See Burton L. Mack with Vernon K. Robbins, *Patterns of Persuasion in the New Testament* (Santa Rosa, Calif.: Polebridge Press, 1999), p. 141, for more on the general lack of closure in Mark's syllogisms. Mark clearly thinks the human world is tragic, not logical.

18. Admittedly, Mark does tell us in his very first sentence that Jesus was in the wilderness "being tested [*peirazomenos*] by Satan," but the point is that this is all he says. There is no concrete, threefold temptation narrative as we find it in Matthew and in Luke. Is it possible that Gethsemane, with its triple repetition of the prayer, represents Mark's very distinctive understanding of what it means for a Christian to be tempted?

19. Simone Weil, "L'Iliade, ou le Poème de la Force," in *La Source Grecque* (Paris: Gallimard, 1953), p. 27; my translation.

20. Most commentators on Mark's gospel do not deal with this scene because it is so short and so strange. It is often related to the final scene in the gospel (Mark 16:5–6), if only because the same "young man" (*neaniskos*) appears again. See Robin Scroggs and Kent Groff, "Baptism in Mark: Dying and Rising with Christ," *Journal of Biblical*

Literature, 1973, *92,* 542, but also see John Dominic Crossan, *Four Other Gospels: Shadows on the Contours of the Canon* (Minneapolis, Minn.: Winston, 1985), pp. 91–124, and Frank Kermode, *The Genesis of Secrecy,* pp. 55–65, for views closer to mine. Crossan has also argued that the empty tomb really lies at the heart of Mark's concern for the experience of God's absence. Neither God nor Jesus is "here" in any "place" to which the first-century Christian, or we, can point. Crossan goes on to argue that this was a pointed message to the naively optimistic Christians of Mark's own day, with their simple assumption that Jesus is present, whether at table with them in the Eucharist or in the trials and tribulations of martyrdom. See John Dominic Crossan, "Empty Tomb and Absent Lord," in Werner Kelber (ed.), *The Passion in Mark* (Minneapolis, Minn.: Augsburg Fortress, 1976), pp. 135–152, and Crossan's follow-up article, "A Form of Absence: The Marcan Creation of Gospel," *SEMEIA,* 1978, *12,* 41–55. Finally, see Vernon K. Robbins, "Last Meal: Preparation, Betrayal, and Absence," in *The Passion in Mark,* pp. 35–38.

21. Christopher Burdon, *Stumbling on God: Faith and Vision Through Mark's Gospel* (Grand Rapids, Mich.: Eerdmans, 1990), p. 79.

22. See Raymond E. Brown; "The Passion According to Mark," *Worship,* 1985, *59,* 118, 124.

23. This all-purpose Greek word, often translated as "study," gives us a great many modern technical terms: *geology, psychology, anthropology, theology,* and so on. Here it means not so much "study" as a "giving of an account." John's evangel begins by suggesting that the *Logos* became incarnate in a human body, difficult as this is to comprehend. We are expected to wonder if this incarnate *Logos* may in fact be Jesus. In the early 1500s, Erasmus of Rotterdam famously translated the first line of John this way: "In the beginning was the *conversation.*" Chinese theologians in the 1960s translated it as "In the beginning was *the Tao.*" You see the point and its complexity.

24. This and all the other noncanonical gospels may be found in James M. Robinson (ed.), *The Nag Hammadi Library* (New York: HarperCollins, 1977); see pp. 339–345, esp. p. 344.

25. See Rodolphe Kasser, Marvin Meyer, and Gregor Wurst (eds.), *The Gospel of Judas* (Washington, D.C.: National Geographic, 2006), pp. 19–45, as well as Elaine Pagels and Karen L. King, *Reading Judas: The Gospel of Judas and the Shaping of Early Christianity* (New York: Random House, 2007). The codex containing this gospel was discovered in a bookseller's stall in Egypt in the 1970s and stored in several very strange locations, from a safe deposit box on Long Island to the freezer in someone's personal refrigerator (which nearly destroyed it). Today it resides in Basel, Switzerland.

26. Kasser, Meyer, and Wurst, *Gospel of Judas,* p. 43.

27. For a useful discussion of the variety of Hebrew phrases rendered in the Septuagint as *egô eimi,* see Raymond E. Brown, *The Gospel According to John: "The Anchor Bible,"* Vol. 29 (New York: Doubleday, 1966), pp. 533–538. For a more concrete discussion of the function of the phrase in this particular setting, see pp. 817–818 of Vol. 29A. I'll have more to say about this phrase in Chapter Four.

28. For more on the garden imagery and its theological juxtapositions, see my *God Gardened East* (Eugene, Ore.: Wipf & Stock, 2007). B. P. Robinson suggests, in "Gethsemane: The Synoptic and the Johannine Viewpoints," *Church Quarterly Review,* 1966, *167,* 5–7, that John often consciously inverts Jewish symbolism in his evangel.

29. For a very helpful analysis of the anti-Jewish polemics in John, see J. Louis Martyn, *History and Theology in the Fourth Gospel* (Nashville, Tenn.: Parthenon Press, 1968). In a different vein, see Richard L. Rubenstein, "Religion and the Origin of the Death Camps: A Psychoanalytic Interpretation," in *After Auschwitz: History, Theology, and Contemporary Judaism,* 2nd ed. (Baltimore: Johns Hopkins University Press, 1992), pp. 29–61.

30. In a subsequent passage, Jesus offers a curious rationale for "putting up the sword": "My kingdom is not of this world; if my kingdom were of this world, then my followers would fight, so that I should not be handed over to the Jews. But my kingdom is not like this" (John 18:36). The idea that Christians do not belong in the world creates a thicket of new trouble for any Christian who does in fact live in the world—as all of them do, of course.

31.   Dan O. Via Jr., *The Ethics of Mark's Gospel in the Middle of Time* (Minneapolis, Minn.: Augsburg Fortress, 1985), pp. 186–192.

Chapter Three

1.   The Greek text of this poem, *Christos Paschon: Tragôdia,* which was composed by Gregory of Nazianzus (329–389 C.E., nicknamed "the Theologian" by his peers), may be found in J.-P. Migne (ed.), *Patrologiae Graecae: Cursus Completus* (Paris, 1862), Vol. 38, pp. 133–338. Amazingly, it has never been translated into English.

2.   A fascinating story about schooling in Gregory's time may be found in Edward J. Watts, *City and School in Late Antique Athens and Alexandria* (Berkeley: University of California Press, 2006), esp. pp. 63–64.

3.   One ancient Christian tradition suggests that Matthew was originally written in Aramaic and later translated. The trouble is that we don't have the original, if it really existed; all we have is the Greek version. Irenaeus is our earliest source for this tradition. See his *Against Heresies* III.1 in Cyril R. Richardson (ed.), *Early Christian Fathers* (New York: Palgrave Macmillan, 1970), p. 370. See also Eusebius, *Ecclesiastical History* III.24.6.

4.   Plato, *Symposium,* 223d.

5.   Walter Kerr, *Tragedy and Comedy* (New York: Simon & Schuster, 1967), p. 2.

6.   Two especially important studies are Peter Szondi, *An Essay on the Tragic,* trans. Paul Fleming (Stanford, Calif.: Stanford University Press, 2002), and Vassilis Lambropoulos, *The Tragic Idea* (London: Duckworth, 2006).

7.   For a longer explanation of Hegel's views on tragedy that I will discuss briefly here, see my first book, *Tragic Posture and Tragic Vision: Against the Modern Failure of Nerve* (New York: Continuum, 1994), pp. 71–127.

8.   See the especially valuable collection of Hegel's scattered reflections on tragedy in Henry Paolucci and Anne Paolucci (eds.), *Hegel on Tragedy* (New York: HarperCollins, 1962).

9.   Edith Hamilton, *The Greek Way* (New York: Norton, 1930), p. 156.

10. Clark Butler (ed.), *Hegel: The Letters* (Bloomington: Indiana University Press, 1984), p. 57.

11. See my essay "Nietzsche, the Death of God, and Truth, or, Why I Still Like Reading Nietzsche," *Journal of the American Academy of Religion,* 1997, *65,* 573–585; see also my *Tragic Posture and Tragic Vision,* pp. 128–180.

12. Friedrich Nietzsche, *The Birth of Tragedy,* sec. 9.

13. Aristotle, *Poetics,* 1449b25–28.

14. Aristotle, *Poetics*, 1449b13–15.

15. Aristotle, *Poetics*, 1450b26.

16. This last phrase appears in various ways: it is "Son of God" in most of the oldest manuscripts, "the Son of God" in others, and "Son of the Lord" in one medieval manuscript. Many important early Christian thinkers, including Irenaeus, Origen, Basil, Cyrus of Jerusalem, Epiphanius, and Jerome, all quote this verse without this phrase, which is most odd.

17. See Susan Garrett, *The Temptations of Jesus in Mark's Gospel* (Grand Rapids, Mich.: Eerdmans, 1998).

18. Nietzsche famously quipped in *Beyond Good and Evil,* no. 121, "It was clever of God to learn Greek when he wanted to become a storyteller—and that he didn't learn it better."

19. See William Farmer, *The Last Twelve Verses of Mark* (New York: Cambridge University Press, 1974), as well as my *Tragic Posture and Tragic Vision,* pp. 248–255.

20. I extend this analogy in greater detail in *Tragic Posture and Tragic Vision,* pp. 181–198.

Chapter Four

1. See especially David Friedrich Strauss, *The Life of Jesus Critically Examined,* trans. George Eliot (Minneapolis, Minn.: Augsburg Fortress, 1973; originally published 1835), and *The Old Faith and the New,* trans. Mathilde Blind (Amherst, N.Y.: Prometheus, 1997; originally published 1873).

2. See Nietzsche's essay, "David Strauss: Writer and Confessor," trans. Herbert Golder, in William Arrowmsith (ed.), *Unmodern Observations* (New Haven, Conn.: Yale University Press, 1990), pp. 3–72, as well as "Raids of an Untimely Man," no. 5, in *Twilight of the Idols,* trans. Richard Polt (Indianapolis, Ind.: Hackett, 1997), pp. 53–54. See also Albert Schweitzer, *The Quest for the Historical Jesus: A Critical Study of Its Progress from Reimarus to Wrede,* trans. James M. Robinson (New York: Palgrave Macmillan, 1968), pp. 68–120.

3. E. R. Goodenough, "John: A Primitive Gospel," *Journal of Biblical Literature,* 1945, *64,* 145–182; William Foxwell Albright, "Recent Discoveries in Palestine and the Gospel of St. John," in W. D. Davies and David Daube (eds.), *The Background of the New Testament and Its Eschatology* (New York: Cambridge University Press, 1956), pp. 153–171.

4. Benjamin Wisner Bacon, *The Fourth Gospel in Research and Debate* (New York: Moffatt, Yard, 1910), p. 368.

5. Benjamin Wisner Bacon, *The Gospel of the Hellenes* (New York: Cambridge University Press, 1933).

6. P. Gardner-Smith, *Saint John and the Synoptic Gospels* (New York: Cambridge University Press, 1938).

7. J. T. Sanders, *The New Testament Christological Hymns: Their Historical Religious Background* (New York: Cambridge University Press, 1971), pp. 20–57.

8. See Gregory Riley, *Resurrection Reconsidered: Thomas and John in Controversy* (Minneapolis: University of Minnesota Press, 1995).

9. See Ann Graham Brock, *Mary Magdalene, the First Apostle: The Struggle for Authority* (Cambridge, Mass.: Harvard Divinity School, 2003), pp. 55–60.

10. Bart D. Ehrman, *Misquoting Jesus: The Story of Who Changed the Bible and Why* (San Francisco: HarperOne, 2005), pp. 62–65.

11. The oldest gospel manuscripts, including the *Codex Sinaiticus,* omit John 7:53–8:11 altogether, and early Christian writers like Clement, Tertullian, Origen, Cyprian, Chrysostom, Nonnus, and Cyril of Jerusalem do not mention the story when we might expect

them to do so. Even Jerome and Augustine are confused by the story and jumble it up.

12. As I have already shown, Mark and Matthew report that Jesus quoted an agonizing moment from the first line of Psalm 22: "My God, my God, why have you abandoned me?" at the end of his life, and Luke reports that Jesus simply resigned himself to his destiny with the following: "Father, into your hands I commit my spirit."

13. See Gregory Riley, *Resurrection Reconsidered,* and Elaine Pagels, *Beyond Belief: The Secret Gospel of Thomas* (New York: Random House, 2003), pp. 57–58.

14. See Glenn W. Most, *Doubting Thomas* (Cambridge, Mass.: Harvard University Press, 2007), pp. 28–68.

15. The earliest Christian martyr whose own words we have—a man named Ignatius, the bishop of Antioch, who may have been killed around the year 110 C.E.—made this connection between John's antiworldliness and Christian martyrdom explicit: "Christianity is not the work of persuasion, but of greatness, and best when it is hated by the world" (*Letter to the Romans* 3.3). For the Greek text of Ignatius's letters, I am using Bart D. Ehrman (ed.), *Apostolic Fathers,* Vol. 1 (Cambridge, Mass.: Harvard University Press, 2003), pp. 272–273.

Chapter Five

1. The notion was that Mark worked mainly in Rome and Alexandria. See Eusebius, *Ecclesiastical History* II.15.1–16.1, II.24, and III.39.12–16.

2. Eusebius, *Ecclesiastical History* II.10.1–2, II.11.1–2, and V.8.1–4.

3. See Eusebius, *Ecclesiastical History* III.24.5 but also III.32.8.

4. If retrospect confers an advantage to believers, as I contend, then the Nag Hammadi Library is of interest not only to scholars of early Christian history. If modern Christians are serious about their traditions and their history, then these other gospels, now widely available in English, should be as widely read in Bible study groups as they currently are in seminaries and universities and even the Vatican.

5. A recent book suggests that this changing technology of book production inspired Christians to imagine whole new genres and new techniques of writing. See Anthony Grafton and Megan Williams, *Christianity and the Transformation of the Book: Origen, Eusebius, and the Library of Caesarea* (Cambridge, Mass.: Harvard University Press, 2006).

6. Plato, *Republic,* 588b–589b.

7. See, for example, C. K. Barrett (ed.), *The New Testament Background: Selected Documents,* rev. ed. (San Francisco: HarperOne, 1987; originally published 1956), pp. 92–103; Rudolf Bultmann, *Primitive Christianity in Its Contemporary Setting,* trans. R. H. Fuller (New York: Meridian Books, 1956), pp. 103–171; Hans Jonas, *The Gnostic Religion* (Boston: Beacon Press, 1958); and Adolf von Harnack, *The Mission and Expansion of Christianity in the First Three Centuries,* trans. James Moffatt (New York: HarperCollins, 1961), pp. 93–100, 312–318. There is even an ancient Neoplatonic quarrel with Gnosticism, available in Plotinus's *Enneads* 2, ch. 9, ed. A. H. Armstrong (Cambridge, Mass.: Loeb Classical Library, Harvard University Press, 2001; originally published 1966).

8. A more recent survey of this material in light of the Nag Hammadi discoveries is Karen King, *What Is Gnosticism?* (Cambridge, Mass.: Harvard University Press, 2003).

9. Eusebius, *Ecclesiastical History* II.1.4, reports this tradition most clearly.

10. See the helpful discussion in Pagels, *Beyond Belief,* pp. 115–135.

11. Recall that the disciples were afraid that Jesus was a "spirit" (*pneuma*) when they first saw him after his rising, according to Luke.

12. See "The Interpretation of Knowledge" and "A Valentinian Exposition," trans. Elaine Pagels and John D. Turner, in James M. Robinson (ed.), *The Nag Hammadi Library* (San Francisco: HarperOne, 1977), pp. 427–442.

13. Although Origen wrote extensively against the "Gnostics," his very similar Neoplatonic views are clearest in *On First Principles,* trans. G. W. Butterworth (Gloucester, Mass.: Peter Smith, 1973), a text

that tells much the same story (esp. bk. 1, chs. 1–3, pp. 1–39) and later got him into trouble. The early Church never could fully make up its mind about Origen's orthodoxy.

14. Two English versions of the Gospel of Mary are available, in Robinson, *Nag Hammadi Library,* pp. 471–474, and in Robert J. Miller (ed.), *The Complete Gospels* (Santa Rosa, Calif.: Polebridge Press, 1992), pp. 351–360. In addition, see the excellent discussion of these texts in Brock, *Mary Magdalene,* pp. 81–86, and Marvin Meyer, *The Gospels of Mary: The Secret Tradition of Mary Magdalene, the Companion of Jesus* (San Francisco: HarperOne, 2004).

15. Miller, *Complete Gospels,* pp. 323–333.

16. The Gospel of Mary, sec. 4, in Miller, *Complete Gospels,* p. 356.

17. The Gospel of Mary, sec. 6, in Miller, *Complete Gospels,* p. 357.

18. The Gospel of Mary, sec. 10, in Miller, *Complete Gospels,* p. 359.

19. Maybe more, depending on how you viewed the canonical status of the books called Maccabees, Tobit, Judith, Susanna, Bel and the Dragon, and the like. For more on these complex scriptural matters, see Bruce M. Metzger, *An Introduction to the Apocrypha* (New York: Oxford University Press, 1957).

20. Martin Luther cast doubt on the very idea of such councils in his rejection of a great deal of churchly authority. Luther can sound a lot like Valentinus, as we will see in Chapter Six. And like Valentinus, Luther preferred John's evangel to the rest. See Martin Luther, "On the Councils and the Church," in Timothy F. Lull (ed.), *Martin Luther's Basic Theological Writings* (Minneapolis, Minn.: Augsburg Fortress, 1989), pp. 540–575.

21. Robinson, *Nag Hammadi Library,* pp. 339–345.

22. The Greek and English text of Barnabas's letter may be found in Ehrman, *Apostolic Fathers,* Volume 2, pp. 1–83.

23. The Greek and English text of the Shepherd of Hermas may be found in Ehrman, *Apostolic Fathers,* Vol. 2, pp. 161–473.

24. See Harry Y. Gamble Jr., "Christianity: Scripture and Canon," in Frederick M. Denny and Rodney L. Taylor (eds.), *The Holy Book*

in Comparative Perspective (Columbia: University of South Carolina Press, 1985), pp. 36–62, as well as Jonathan Z. Smith, "Sacred Persistence: Toward a Redescription of Canon," in *Imagining Religion: From Babylon to Jonestown* (Chicago: University of Chicago Press, 1982), pp. 36–52.

25. An important second- or third-century document elaborating this structure is Hippolytos's *On the Apostolic Tradition,* trans. Alistair Stewart-Sykes (Crestwood, N.Y.: Saint Vladimir's Seminary Press, 2001).

26. See Origen's *Commentary on John,* 1:4–9 and 10:2–4, in Alan Menzies (ed.), *Ante-Nicene Fathers,* 4th ed. (Peabody, Mass.: Hendrickson, 1995), Vol. 9, pp. 298–302, 381–384. It is important to note that Origen was already convinced that John's was the most important "gospel" precisely because it was so "spiritual."

27. I have little interest in contemporary debates about "fundamentalism" or the "inerrancy of scripture," terms far too imprecise to be worth arguing over. The point is that no one in the fourth century talked about or imagined scripture in this way. That is a *modern* preoccupation, made possible in large part by the invention of the printing press, and the ever more individualist religious revolution embodied in the Protestant Reformation.

28. An English translation of the *Diatessaron* may be found in Menzies, *Ante-Nicene Fathers,* Vol. 9, pp. 35–138. For more on the importance of this document, see Tjitze Baarda, " $\Delta IA\Phi\Omega NIA$-$\Sigma YM\Phi\Omega NIA$: Factors in the Harmonization of the Gospels, Especially in the Diatessaron of Tatian," in W. L. Peterson (ed.), *Gospel Traditions in the Second Century: Origins, Recensions, Text and Transmission* (Notre Dame, Ind.: University of Notre Dame Press, 1989), pp. 133–154, for some interesting general theories about this "gospel harmony." First and foremost, Baarda suggests that John's gospel was originally more popular in Rome and Alexandria than anywhere in the Christian East. Since he received his Christian training in Rome, Tatian was required to deal with four gospels, not three. Moreover, Tatian was quarreling with some pagan polemicists, like Celsus, who used apparent discrepancies in the Christian scriptures to condemn the

whole Christian movement. Tatian's answer to such pagan complaints was to suggest that such inconsistencies were apparent and not real. A wonderful summary of what we know about the *Diatessaron* may be found in W. L. Peterson, *Tatian's Diatessaron: Its Creation, Dissemination, Significance, and History in Scholarship* (Leiden, Netherlands: Brill, 1994). Eusebius mentions this *Diatessaron,* one of the few of Tatian's writings he approves, in *Ecclesiastical History* IV.29.6–7.

29. Athanasius's thirty-ninth "Festal Letter" may be found in Archibald Robertson (ed.), *Nicene and Post-Nicene Fathers* (Peabody, Mass.: Hendrickson, 1995), Vol. 4, pp. 551–552. It is interesting to note that even Athanasius admits that other prominent books in the Christian codices can and should be read but that they do not belong on the "official" list. Among these he mentions the Wisdom of Solomon, Sirach, Esther, Judith, Tobit, and the Shepherd of Hermas.

30. Pagels, *Beyond Belief,* pp. 97, 176–177. See also Bart D. Ehrman, *Lost Christianities: The Battle for Scripture and the Faiths We Never Knew* (New York: Oxford University Press, 2003), pp. 54–55.

31. Athanasius, *The Life of Antony and the Letter to Marcellinus,* trans. Robert C. Gregg (Mahwah, N.J.: Paulist Press, 1980).

32. See Melito of Sardis, *On Pascha,* trans. Alistair Stewart-Sykes (Crestwood, N.Y.: Saint Vladimir's Seminary Press, 2001).

33. Materials from all seven may be found in Henry R. Percival (ed.), *Nicene and Post-Nicene Fathers,* 2nd ser. (Peabody, Mass.: Hendrickson, 1995), Vol. 14.

34. For more on this fascinating material, see John of Damascus, *On the Divine Images,* trans. David Anderson (Crestwood, N.Y.: Saint Vladimir's Seminary Press, 1997), and Theodore the Studite, *On the Holy Icons,* trans. Catherine P. Roth (Crestwood, N.Y.: Saint Vladimir's Seminary Press, 1981). Finally, see my *Was Greek Thought Religious? On the Use and Abuse of Hellenism, from Rome to Romanticism* (New York: Palgrave Macmillan, 2002), pp. 77–91.

35. Hippolytos suggests as much in *On the Apostolic Tradition,* "On Bishops," pp. 56–60.

36. The Creed was later expanded to include further discussion of this Holy Spirit. It was provisionally approved in 381 C.E. at the Council of Constantinople but became fully credal in 451 C.E. at the Council of Chalcedon. The Holy Spirit is

 > the Lord and life-creator who proceeded from the Father [the Latin translation of this Creed added the suspect phrase *filoque,* "and from the Son"]; who is worshiped and glorified with the Father and the Son; who spoke through the prophets.

 > And in one holy catholic and apostolic church. I acknowledge one baptism for the remission of sins. And I look forward to the rising up of the dead and life in the world to come. Amen.

37. The two Greek terms used in this debate and in the Nicene Creed were *homo-ousios* ("same substance") and *homoi-ousios* ("similar substance"), resulting in the quip even at the time that this whole theological war hinged on a single letter, the Greek iota.

38. John of Damascus, *The Fount of Wisdom,* in Frederic H. Chase Jr., trans., *Saint John of Damascus: Writings* (Washington, D.C.: Catholic University Press of America, 1958), p. 111.

Chapter Six

1. For a summary of this imperial legislation, see Clyde Pharr (ed.), *The Theodosian Code and Novels and the Sirndonian Contributions* (Princeton, N.J.: Princeton University Press, 1952), pp. 440–476.

2. Tertullian, *De Praescriptione Haereticorum* 7.9.

3. In a similar vein, and primarily aimed at Plato, Tertullian referred to (Greek) philosophers as "patriarchs of the heretics," in his *De Anima* 3.1.

4. Tertullian addressed this most explicitly in *De Spectaculis,* or "On Spectacles," in *Tertullian: Disciplinary, Moral and Ascetical Works* (New York: Fathers of the Church, 1959), Vol. 40, pp. 33–107. Chrysostom has some fascinating comments on related themes in his *Discourse on Blessed Babylas and Against the Greeks,* trans. Margaret

A. Schatkin (Washington, D.C.: Catholic University of America Press, 1983), (secs. 73–80, 114–118), pp. 117–125, 143–151.

5. For a superb summary of the final closure of the Athenian school, see Edward J. Watts, *City and School,* pp. 131–142.

6. His Greek name was Hieronymus, later Latinized as Jerome. He was originally from the Dalmatian coast of Croatia, studied in Rome, and then joined a monastery in Bethlehem for the majority of his long life.

7. Erasmus's given name was Gerrit Gerritszoon, the illegitimate son of the father after whom he was named. After studying in Paris, he worked in England for a short time and slightly longer in North Italy but mostly in Switzerland.

8. See Jan Krans, *Beyond What Is Written: Erasmus and Beza as Conjectural Critics of the New Testament* (Leiden, Netherlands: Brill, 2006).

9. See Bruce Mansfield, *Erasmus in the Twentieth Century* (Toronto: University of Toronto Press, 2003).

10. See Luther's 1530 essay "On Translation: An Open Letter," trans. Charles M. Jacobs, in E. Theodore Bachmann (ed.), *Luther's Works,* Vol. 35 (Philadelphia: Muehlenberg Press, 1960), pp. 175–202.

11. Martin Luther, "Sermons on Genesis, Chapters 15–20," in Jaroslav Pelikan (ed.), *Luther's Works,* Vol. 3 (Saint Louis, Mo.: Concordia, 1961), p. 113.

12. Franklin Sherman (ed.), *Luther's Works,* trans. Martin H. Berman, Vol. 47 (Minneapolis, Minn.: Augsburg Fortress, 1971), pp. 123–306.

13. Martin Luther, "On the Jews and Their Lies," in Sherman, *Luther's Works,* Vol. 47, pp. 139–140.

14. See Exodus 7:3, 9:12, 10:20, 10:27, 14:4, and 14:17, but see also, on the other hand, Exodus 7:13–14, 8:15, 8:32, 9:27, 10:16, and 13:15.

15. Martin Luther, "Sermons," in Hans J. Hillebrand (ed.), *Luther's Works,* Vol. 52 (Minneapolis, Minn.: Augsburg Fortress, 1974), pp. 177–178.

16. Martin Luther, "Sermon on the Sermon on the Mount," in Jaroslav Pelikan (ed.), *Luther's Works,* Vol. 21 (Saint Louis, Mo.: Concordia, 1956), p. 65. Here is the clearest example of how the Protestant return to

"scripture alone" helped make modern biblical criticism possible. If Luther can distinguish between Mark's gospel and John's evangel, and if he can clearly discern their contradictory interests, then so can Erasmus or David Strauss or any of us who read these same scriptures today.

17. Even the community of Bible translators hired by King James in England in 1611 did so. Their preface, addressed to the king, is rarely included in contemporary editions of the so-called King James Bible, almost as if the editors do not wish to remind us that the book was a new translation of works originally written in other languages and that at the time it was published, it was a brand-new version, not a "traditional" one at all.

18. Martin Luther, "Preface to His Translation of the New Testament," in Bachmann, *Luther's Works,* Vol. 35, pp. 361–362.

19. Martin Luther, "Sermons on the Gospel of John, Chapters 6–8," in Jaroslav Pelikan (ed.), *Luther's Works,* Vol. 23 (Saint Louis, Mo.: Concordia, 1959), p. 77.

20. These marble steps served as the main entrance to the papal palace in Luther's day. Tradition held that prayers offered on these steps could help intercede for the souls held in purgatory, and Luther offered up his own. In 1586, Pope Sixtus V commissioned a total reconstruction of the Lateran complex. Thus, the "sacred steps" are now housed in a separate building, covered in walnut wood for their protection, and may be used only by pilgrims who ascend them on their knees.

This strange story was told in a homily that Luther delivered on November 15, 1545, and that was rediscovered by G. Buchwald, who first reported its discovery in 1911 in the *Wissenschaftliche Beilage der Leipziger Zeitung.* The part-Latin, part-German text may be found in *D. Martin Luthers Werke* (Weimar: Hermann Böhlaus Nachfolger, 1914), Vol. 51, pp. 87–90 (esp. p. 89). The story has been widely reported by scholars such as Hartmann Grisar, *Luther,* trans. E. M. Lamond (London: Kegan Paul, Trench, Trübner & Co., 1914), Vol. 1, pp. 29–38 (esp. p. 33); Roland Bainton, *Here I Stand: A Life of Martin Luther* (Nashville, Tenn.: Abingdon, 1950), pp. 48–51;

and Martin Marty, *Martin Luther* (New York: Viking Books, 2004), pp. 12–14.

21. George Marsden is the contemporary scholar who has perhaps made this point best. See his *Understanding Fundamentalism and Evangelicalism,* 2nd ed. (Grand Rapids, Mich.: Eerdmans, 1998).

22. Jerry Falwell, with Ed Dobson and Ed Hindson, *The Fundamentalist Phenomenon: The Resurgence of Conservative Christianity* (New York: Doubleday, 1981), p. 37.

SELECTED BIBLIOGRAPHY

Aland, Kurt, Matthew Black, Carlo M. Martini, Bruce M. Metzger, and Allen Wikgren. *The Greek New Testament* (3rd ed.). Münster, Germany: United Bible Societies, 1975.

Athanasius of Alexandria. *The Life of Antony and the Letter to Marcellinus,* trans. Robert C. Gregg. Mahwah, N.J.: Paulist Press, 1980.

Athanassiadi, Polymnia. *Julian: An Intellectual Biography* (rev. ed.). New York: Routledge, 1992.

Ayres, Lewis. *Imagining Jesus: An Introduction to the Incarnation.* London: Affirming Catholicism, 1992.

Ayres, Lewis. *Nicaea and Its Legacy: An Approach to Fourth Century Trinitarian Theology.* Oxford, England: Oxford University Press, 2004.

Ayres, Lewis, with Gareth Jones (eds.). *Christian Origins: Theology, Rhetoric and Community.* London: Routledge, 1998.

Bailey, James L., and Lyle D. Van der Broek. *Literary Forms in the New Testament: A Handbook.* Louisville, Ky.: Westminster/John Knox, 1992.

Bainton, Roland H. *Here I Stand: A Life of Martin Luther.* New York: Meridian, 1995. (Originally published 1950)

Barnhardt, Wilton. *Gospel: A Novel.* New York: Picador, 1993.

Barrett, C. K. *The New Testament Background: Selected Documents* (rev. ed.). New York: HarperCollins, 1987.

Behr, John. *The Nicene Faith.* Crestwood, N.Y.: Saint Vladimir's Seminary Press, 2004.

Bennett, Rod. *Four Witnesses: The Early Church in Her Own Words.* San Francisco: Ignatius Press, 2002.

Berchman, Robert M. *Porphyry: Against the Christians.* Boston: Brill, 2005.

Bilezikian, Gilbert G. *The Liberated Gospel: A Comparison of the Gospel of Mark and Greek Tragedy*. Grand Rapids, Mich.: Baker, 1977.

Bitton-Ashkelony, Brouria. *Encountering the Sacred: The Debate on Christian Pilgrimage in Late Antiquity*. Berkeley: University of California Press, 2005.

Blanton, Ward. *Displacing Christian Origins: Philosophy, Secularity, and the New Testament*. Chicago: University of Chicago Press, 2007.

Bowersock, Glen. *Fiction as History: Nero to Julian*. Berkeley: University of California Press, 1994.

Bowersock, Glen. *Julian the Apostate*. Cambridge, Mass.: Harvard University Press, 1978.

Bowersock, Glen, with Peter Brown and Oleg Grabar. *Interpreting Late Antiquity: Essays on the Postclassical World*. Cambridge, Mass.: Harvard University Press, 2001.

Boyarin, Daniel. *Border Lines: The Idea of Orthodoxy and the Partitioning of Judeo-Christianity*. Philadelphia: University of Pennsylvania Press, 2004.

Brock, Ann Graham. *Mary Magdalene, the First Apostle: The Struggle for Authority*. Cambridge, Mass.: Harvard University Press, 2003.

Brown, Norman O. *Life Against Death: The Psychoanalytical Meaning of History*. Middletown, Conn.: Wesleyan University Press, 1959.

Brown, Peter. *The Body and Society: Men, Women, and Sexual Renunciation in Early Christianity*. New York: Columbia University Press, 1988.

Brown, Peter. *The Cult of the Saints: Its Rise and Function in Latin Christianity*. Chicago: University of Chicago Press, 1981.

Brown, Peter. *The Making of Late Antiquity*. Cambridge, Mass.: Harvard University Press, 1978.

Brown, Peter. *The Rise of Western Christendom: Triumph and Diversity, A.D. 200–1000* (2nd ed.). Malden, Mass.: Blackwell, 2003.

Brown, Raymond E. *The Death of the Messiah: From Gethsemane to the Grave*. New York: New York University Press, 1993.

Brown, Raymond E. *The Gospel According to John: Introduction, Translation, and Notes*. New York: Doubleday, 1966.

Bryan, Christopher. *A Preface to Mark: Notes on the Gospel in Its Literary and Cultural Setting*. New York: Oxford University Press, 1993.

Bull, Malcolm. *The Mirror of the Gods: How Renaissance Artists Rediscovered the Pagan Gods*. New York: Oxford University Press, 2005.

Bultmann, Rudolf. *History of the Synoptic Tradition*, trans. John Marsh. New York: HarperCollins, 1963.

Bultmann, Rudolf. *Jesus Christ and Mythology*. New York: Scribner, 1958.

Bultmann, Rudolf. *Jesus and the Word,* trans. Louise Pettibone Smith and Erminie Huntress Lantero. New York: Scribner, 1958. (Originally published 1934)

Bultmann, Rudolf. *Kerygma and Myth: A Theological Debate,* ed. Hans Werner Bartsch. New York: HarperCollins, 2000. (Originally published 1961)

Bultmann, Rudolf. *Primitive Christianity in Its Contemporary Setting,* trans. R. H. Fuller. New York: Meridian, 1956.

Burdon, Christopher. *Stumbling on God: Faith and Vision Through Mark's Gospel*. Grand Rapids, Mich.: Eerdmans, 1990.

Cameron, Ron (ed.). *The Other Gospels: Non-Canonical Gospel Texts*. Louisville, Ky.: Westminster/John Knox, 1982.

Capon, Robert Farrar. *Between Noon and Three: Romance, Law, and the Outrage of Grace*. Louisville, Ky.: Westminster/John Knox, 1997.

Carroll, John. *The Existential Jesus*. Melbourne, Australia: Scribe, 2007.

Coffin, William Sloane. *Credo*. Louisville, Ky.: Westminster/John Knox, 2004.

Cross, F. L. (ed.). *The Oxford Dictionary of the Christian Church*. New York: Oxford University Press, 1958.

Crossan, John Dominic. *The Birth of Christianity: Beneath the Stones, Behind the Texts*. San Francisco: HarperOne, 2001.

Crossan, John Dominic. *Excavating Jesus: Discovering What Happened in the Years Immediately After the Execution of Jesus*. San Francisco: HarperOne, 1998.

Crossan, John Dominic. *Four Other Gospels: Shadows on the Contour of the Canon*. Minneapolis, Minn.: Winston, 1985.

Culpepper, R. Alan. *Anatomy of the Fourth Gospel: A Study in Literary Design*. Minneapolis, Minn.: Augsburg Fortress, 1983.

Daniel-Reps, H. *The Church of Apostles and Martyrs*. New York: Dutton, 1960.

Davies, J. G. *The Early Christian Church: A History of Its First Five Centuries*. Grand Rapids, Mich.: Baker, 1965.

Denzey, Nicola. *The Bone Gatherers: The Last Worlds of Early Christian Women*. Boston: Beacon Press, 2007.

Dibelius, Martin. *From Tradition to Gospel,* trans. Bertram Lee Woolf. Cambridge, England: Clarke, 1971. (Originally published 1919)

Dodd, Charles H. *The Apostolic Preaching and Its Developments*. Grand Rapids, Mich.: Baker, 1980.

Dodd, Charles H. *Historical Tradition in the Fourth Gospel*. New York: Cambridge University Press, 1963.

Dowd, Sharon Echols. *Prayer, Power, and the Problem of Suffering: Mark 11:22–25 in the Context of Markan Theology*. Atlanta: Society of Biblical Literature, 1988.

Dunderberg, Ismo, Christopher Tuckett, and Kari Syreeni (eds.). *Fair Play: Diversity and Conflicts in Early Christianity*. Boston: Brill, 2002.

Ehrman, Bart D. *Lost Christianities: The Battle for Scripture and the Faiths We Never Knew*. New York: Oxford University Press, 2003.

Ehrman, Bart D. *Misquoting Jesus: Who Changed the Bible and Why*. San Francisco: HarperOne, 2005.

Eusebius of Caesarea. *Ecclesiastical History*, trans. Kirsopp Lane (2 vols.). Cambridge, Mass.: Harvard University Press, 1992.

Eusebius of Caesarea. *The Life of Constantine,* trans. Averil Cameron and Stuart G. Hall. Oxford, England: Oxford University Press, 1999.

Falwell, Jerry. *Listen America!* New York: Doubleday, 1980.

Falwell, Jerry, with Ed Dobson and Ed Hindson (eds.). *The Fundamentalist Phenomenon: The Resurgence of Conservative Christianity*. New York: Doubleday, 1981.

Farmer, William. *The Last Twelve Verses of Mark*. New York: Cambridge University Press, 1974.

Fortna, Robert T. *The Fourth Gospel and Its Predecessor: From Narrative Source to the Present Gospel*. Minneapolis, Minn.: Augsburg Fortress, 1988.

Fortna, Robert T. *The Gospel of Signs: Reconstruction of the Narrative Source Underlying the Fourth Gospel*. New York: Cambridge University Press, 1970.

Fortna, Robert T., with Tom Thatcher (eds.). *Jesus in Johannine Tradition*. Louisville, Ky.: Westminster/John Knox, 2001.

Frend, W.H.C. *The Early Church*. Minneapolis, Minn.: Augsburg Fortress, 1982.

Garrett, Susan R. *The Demise of the Devil: Magic and the Demonic in Luke's Writings*. Minneapolis, Minn.: Augsburg Fortress, 1989.

Garrett, Susan R. *The Temptations of Jesus in Mark's Gospel*. Grand Rapids, Mich.: Eerdmans, 1998.

Goldhill, Simon. *Love, Sex, Tragedy: How the Ancient World Shapes Our Lives*. Chicago: Chicago University Press, 2004.

Grafton, Anthony. *New Worlds, Ancient Texts: The Power of Tradition and the Shock of Discovery*. Cambridge, Mass.: Harvard University Press, 1992.

Greenslade, S. L. (ed.). *Early Latin Theology*. Louisville, Ky.: Westminster/John Knox, 1956.

Gregg, Robert C., and Dennis C. Groh. *Early Arianism: A View of Salvation*. Minneapolis, Minn.: Augsburg Fortress, 1981.

Hardy, Edward R. (ed.). *Christology of the Later Fathers*. Louisville, Ky.: Westminster/John Knox, 1954.

Hargis, Jeffrey W. *Against the Christians: The Rise of Early Anti-Christian Polemic*. New York: Peter Lang, 1999.

Harnack, Adolf von. *The Mission and Expansion of Christianity in the First Three Centuries,* trans. James Moffatt. New York: HarperCollins, 1961.

Harpur, Tom. *The Pagan Christ: Recovering the Lost Light*. New York: Walker, 2004.

Harran, Marilyn J. *Luther on Conversion: The Early Years*. Ithaca, N.Y.: Cornell University Press, 1983.

Hauerwas, Stanley. *The Peaceable Kingdom: A Primer in Christian Ethics*. Notre Dame, Ind.: Notre Dame University Press, 1983.

Hauerwas, Stanley. *Unleashing the Scripture: Freeing the Bible from Captivity to America*. Nashville, Tenn.: Abingdon Press, 1993.

Hegel, G.W.F. *The Phenomenology of Mind*, trans. J. B. Baillie. Atlantic Highlands, N.J.: Humanities Press, 1910.

Hegel, G.W.F. *Lectures on the Philosophy of History*, trans. C. Friedrich. New York: Dover, 1956.

Hegel, G.W.F. *Lectures on the Philosophy of Religion*, ed. Peter C. Hodgson (2 vols.). Berkeley: University of California Press, 1984, 1987.

Hippolytos. *On the Apostolic Tradition,* trans. Alistair Stewart-Sykes. Crestwood, N.Y.: Saint Vladimir's Seminary Press, 2001.

Hoffman, R. Joseph (trans.). *Celsus on the True Doctrine: A Discourse Against the Christians*. Oxford, England: Oxford University Press, 1987.

Hoffman, R. Joseph (trans.). *Julian's Against the Galileans*. Amherst, N.Y.: Prometheus, 2004.

Hoffman, R. Joseph (trans.). *Porphyry's Against the Christians*. Amherst, N.Y.: Prometheus, 1994.

Horsley, Richard A., Jonathan A. Draper, and John Miles Foley (eds.). *Performing the Gospel: Morality, Memory, and Mark*. Minneapolis, Minn.: Augsburg Fortress, 2006.

Jaegar, Werner. *Early Christianity and Greek Paideia*. Cambridge, Mass.: Harvard University Press, 1961.

Johnson, Paul. *The Renaissance: A Short History*. New York: Modern Library, 2000.

Johnson, Scott Fitzgerald. *The Life and Miracles of Thekla: A Literary Study*. Washington, D.C.: Center for Hellenic Studies, 2006.

Jonas, Hans. *The Gnostic Religion*. Boston: Beacon Press, 1958.

Kelber, Werner H. *Mark's Story of Jesus*. Minneapolis, Minn.: Augsburg Fortress, 1979.

Kelber, Werner H. *The Oral and Written Gospel: The Hermeneutics of Speaking and Writing in the Synoptic Tradition, Mark, Paul, and Q* (rev. ed.). Bloomington: Indiana University Press, 1997.

Kelber, Werner H. (ed.). *The Passion in Mark*. Minneapolis, Minn.: Augsburg Fortress, 1976.

Kelly, J.N.D. *Golden Mouth: The Story of John Chrysostom, Ascetic, Preacher, Bishop*. Ithaca, N.Y.: Cornell University Press, 1995.

Kennedy, George A. *New Testament Interpretation Through Rhetorical Criticism*. Raleigh: University of North Carolina Press, 1984.

Kermode, Frank. *The Genesis of Secrecy*. Cambridge, Mass.: Harvard University Press, 1979.

Kermode, Frank. *The Sense of an Ending: Studies in the Theory of Fiction*. Oxford, England: Oxford University Press, 1967.

Kerr, Walter. *The Decline of Pleasure*. New York: Simon & Schuster, 1962.

Kerr, Walter. *How Not to Write a Play*. New York: Simon & Schuster, 1955.

Kerr, Walter. *Tragedy and Comedy*. New York: Simon & Schuster, 1967.

King, Karen. *What Is Gnosticism?* New York: Cambridge University Press, 2003.

Kingsbury, Jack Dean. *The Christology of Mark's Gospel*. Minneapolis, Minn.: Augsburg Fortress, 1983.

Kittelson, James. *Luther the Reformer: The Story of the Man and His Career*. Minneapolis, Minn.: Augsburg Fortress, 1986.

Knust, Jennifer Wright. *Abandoned to Lust: Sexual Slander and Ancient Christianity*. New York: Columbia University Press, 2006.

Koester, Helmut. *Ancient Christian Gospels: Their History and Development*. Harrisburg, Pa.: Trinity Press, 1990.

Koester, Helmut. *Introduction to the New Testament: History and Literature of Early Christianity* (2nd ed.). Hawthorne, N.Y.: Aldine de Gruyter, 2000.

Koester, Helmut, with J. T. Robinson. *Trajectories Through Early Christianity*. Minneapolis, Minn.: Augsburg Fortress, 1971.

Kofsky, Aryeh. *Eusebius of Caesarea Against Paganism*. Boston: Brill, 2000.

Krans, Jan. *Beyond What Is Written: Erasmus and Beza as Conjectural Critics of the New Testament*. Boston: Brill, 2006.

Lambropoulos, Vassilis. *The Rise of Eurocentrism: Anatomy of Interpretation*. Princeton, N.J.: Princeton University Press, 1993.

Lambropoulos, Vassilis. *The Tragic Idea*. London: Duckworth, 2006.

Levi, Anthony. *Renaissance and Reformation: The Intellectual Genesis*. New Haven, Conn.: Yale University Press, 2002.

Lohse, Bernhard. *Martin Luther's Theology: Its Historical and Systematic Development*. Minneapolis, Minn.: Augsburg Fortress, 1999.

MacDonald, Dennis. *Does the New Testament Imitate Homer? Four Cases from the Acts of the Apostles*. New Haven, Conn.: Yale University Press, 2003.

MacDonald, Dennis. *The Homeric Epics and the Gospel of Mark*. New Haven, Conn.: Yale University Press, 2000.

MacGregor, Geddes. *The Nicene Creed Illuminated by Modern Thought*. Grand Rapids, Mich.: Eerdmans, 1980.

Mack, Burton L. *A Myth of Innocence: Mark and Christian Origins*. Minneapolis, Minn.: Augsburg Fortress, 1988.

Mack, Burton L., with Vernon K. Robbins. *Patterns of Persuasion in the New Testament*. Santa Rosa, Calif.: Polebridge Press, 1999.

Mansfield, Bruce. *Erasmus in the Twentieth Century*. Toronto: University of Toronto Press, 2003.

Markus, R. A. *Christianity in the Roman World*. London: Thames & Hudson, 1974.

Marsden, George M. *Fundamentalism and American Culture: The Shaping of 20th Century Evangelicalism, 1870–1925*. Oxford, England: Oxford University Press, 2006.

Marsden, George M. *Understanding Fundamentalism and Evangelicalism*. Grand Rapids, Mich.: Eerdmans, 1998.

Marthaler, Bernard L. *The Creed*. New London, Conn.: Twenty-Third Publications, 1987.

Martin, Dale B., and Patricia Cox Miller (eds.). *The Cultural Turn in Late Ancient Studies*. Durham, N.C.: Duke University Press, 2005.

Marty, Martin. *Martin Luther*. New York: Viking, 2004.

Martyn, J. Louis. *History and Theology in the Fourth Gospel* (rev. ed.). Nashville, Tenn.: Abingdon Press, 1968.

Marxsen, Willi. *Mark the Evangelist: Studies in the Redaction History of the Gospel,* trans. James Boyce, Donald Juel, and William Poehlman. Nashville, Tenn.: Abingdon Press, 1969.

Mayer, Wendy, and Pauline Allen. *John Chrysostom.* New York: Routledge, 2000.

McCowen, Alec. *Personal Mark: An Actor's Proclamation of Mark's Gospel.* New York: Continuum, 1985.

Mignolo, Walter. *The Darker Side of the Renaissance: Literacy, Territoriality, and Colonization.* Ann Arbor: University of Michigan Press, 1995.

Miller, Robert J., and Robert Funk (eds.). *The Complete Gospels* (2 vols.). Santa Rosa, Calif.: Polebridge Press, 1992, 1994.

Most, Glenn W. *Doubting Thomas.* Cambridge, Mass.: Harvard University Press, 2005.

Myer, Marvin. *Secret Gospels.* Berkeley: University of California Press, 2003.

Myers, Ched. *Binding the Strong Man: A Political Reading of Mark's Story of Jesus.* Oceanside, Calif.: Orbis, 1988.

Negri, Gaetano. *Julian the Apostate*, trans. Litta Visconte Arese. London: Unwin, 1905.

Nestingen, James A. *Martin Luther: A Life.* Minneapolis, Minn.: Augsburg Fortress, 2003.

Nietzsche, Friedrich. *The Birth of Tragedy and the Case of Wagner*, trans. Walter Kaufmann. New York: Vintage Books, 1967.

Nietzsche, Friedrich. *Twilight of the Idols*, trans. Richard Polt. Indianapolis, Ind.: Hackett, 1997.

Norman, A. F. (ed.). *Libanius: The Julian Orations.* Cambridge, Mass.: Harvard University Press, 1969.

Norris, Richard (trans. and ed.). *The Christological Controversy.* Minneapolis, Minn.: Augsburg Fortress, 1980.

Oberman, Heiko A. *Luther: Man Between God and the Devil.* New Haven, Conn.: Yale University Press, 1989.

Pabel, H. M., and M. Vessey (eds.). *Holy Scripture Speaks: The Production and Reception of Erasmus' Paraphrases on the New Testament.* Toronto: University of Toronto Press, 2002.

Pagels, Elaine. *Adam, Eve, and the Serpent*. New York: Vintage Books, 1988.

Pagels, Elaine. *Beyond Belief: The Secret Gospel of Thomas*. New York: Random House, 2003.

Pagels, Elaine. *The Gnostic Gospels*. New York: Vintage Books, 1979.

Pagels, Elaine. *The Gnostic Paul: Gnostic Exegesis of the Pauline Letters*. Harrisburg, Pa.: Trinity Press, 1975.

Pagels, Elaine. *The Johannine Gospel in Gnostic Exegesis*. Nashville, Tenn.: Abingdon Press, 1973.

Pagels, Elaine, and Karen L. King. *Reading Judas: The Gospel of Judas and the Shaping of Early Christianity*. New York: Random House, 2007.

Paolucci, Anne, and Henry Paolucci (eds.). *Hegel on Tragedy*. New York: HarperCollins, 1962.

Paolucci, Henry (ed.). *Hegel on the Arts*. New York: Ungar, 1979.

Pelikan, Jaroslav. *The Christian Tradition: The Emergence of the Catholic Tradition* (3 vols.). Chicago: University of Chicago Press, 1971.

Pelikan, Jaroslav. *Jesus Through the Centuries*. New Haven, Conn.: Yale University Press, 1985.

Pelikan, Jaroslav. *Mary Through the Centuries*. New Haven, Conn.: Yale University Press, 1996.

Pollard, T. E. *Johannine Christianity and the Early Church*. New York: Cambridge University Press, 1970.

Rhoads, David, and Donald Michie. *Mark as Story: An Introduction to the Narrative of a Gospel*. Minneapolis, Minn.: Augsburg Fortress, 1982.

Ricciotti, Giuseppe. *Julian the Apostate*, trans. M. Joseph Costelloe. Milwaukee, Wis.: Bruce, 1960.

Richardson, Cyril C. (ed.). *Early Christian Fathers*. New York: Palgrave Macmillan, 1970.

Riley, Greg. *Resurrection Reconsidered: Thomas and John in Controversy*. Minneapolis: University of Minnesota Press, 1995.

Robbins, Vernon K. *Jesus the Teacher: A Socio-Rhetorical Interpretation of Mark's Gospel* (rev. ed.). Minneapolis, Minn.: Augsburg Fortress, 1992.

Robbins, Vernon K. *The Tapestry of Early Christian Discourse: Rhetoric, Society, and Ideology*. New York: Routledge, 1996.

Robinson, James M. "The Discovery of the Nag Hammadi Codices." *Biblical Archaeologist*, 1979, *42*, 206–224.

Robinson, James M. (ed.). *The Nag Hammadi Library*. New York: HarperCollins, 1977.

Segal, Alan F. *Paul the Convert: The Apostolate and Apostasy of Saul the Pharisee*. New Haven, Conn.: Yale University Press, 1990.

Segal, Alan F. *Rebecca's Children: Judaism and Christianity in the Roman World*. Cambridge, Mass.: Harvard University Press, 1986.

Spivey, Robert A., and D. Moody Smith Jr. *Anatomy of the New Testament: A Guide to Its Structure and Meaning*. New York: Palgrave Macmillan, 1974.

Ruprecht, Louis A., Jr. *Afterwords: Hellenism, Modernism and the Myth of Decadence*. Albany: State University of New York Press, 1996.

Ruprecht, Louis A., Jr. *God Gardened East: A Gardener's Meditation on the Dynamics of Genesis*. Eugene, Ore.: Wipf & Stock, 2007.

Ruprecht, Louis A., Jr. "The Gospel as Tragedy: On Moral Collisions, Tragic Flaws, and the Possibility of Redemption." In Frederick E. Glennon, Gary S. Hauk, and Darryll M. Trimiew, *Living Responsibly in Community: Essays in Honor of E. Clinton Gardner* (pp. 45–68). Lanham, Md.: University Press of America, 1997.

Ruprecht, Louis A., Jr. "Mark's Tragic Vision: Gethsemane," *Religion and Literature*, 1992, *24*(3), 1–25.

Ruprecht, Louis A., Jr. *Tragic Posture and Tragic Vision: Against the Modern Failure of Nerve*. New York: Continuum, 1994.

Ruprecht, Louis A., Jr. *Was Greek Thought Religious? On the Use and Abuse of Hellenism, from Rome to Romanticism*. New York: Palgrave Macmillan, 2002.

Salisbury, Joyce E. *Perpetua's Passion: The Death of a Young Roman Woman*. New York: Routledge, 1997.

Schweitzer, Albert. *The Quest of the Historical Jesus*, trans. James M. Robinson. New York: Palgrave Macmillan, 1968.

Schweizer, Edward. *The Good News According to Mark*, trans. Donald H. Madvig. Louisville, Ky.: Westminster/John Knox, 1970.

Screech, M. A. *Laughter at the Foot of the Cross*. Boulder, Colo.: Westview Press, 1997.

Smith, D. Moody. *Johannine Christianity: Essays on Its Setting, Sources, and Theology*. Columbia: University of South Carolina Press, 1984.

Stout, Jeffrey. *Democracy and Tradition*. Princeton, N.J.: Princeton University Press, 2004.

Stout, Jeffrey. *Ethics After Babel: The Languages of Morals and Their Discontents*. Boston: Beacon Press, 1988.

Stout, Jeffrey. *The Flight from Authority*. Notre Dame, Ind.: Notre Dame University Press, 1981.

Stratton, Kimberly B. *Naming the Witch: Magic, Ideology, and Stereotype in the Ancient World*. New York: Columbia University Press, 2007.

Streeter, Burnett Hillman. *The Four Gospels: A Study of Origins*. New York: Palgrave Macmillan, 1924.

Studer, Basil. *Trinity and Incarnation: The Faith of the Early Church*. New York: Continuum, 1993.

Szondi, Peter. *An Essay on the Tragic*, trans. Paul Fleming. Stanford, Calif.: Stanford University Press, 2002.

Talbert, Charles H. *What Is a Gospel? The Genre of the Canonical Gospels*. Minneapolis, Minn.: Augsburg Fortress, 1977.

Taylor, Vincent. *The Gospel According to Saint Mark*. New York: Palgrave Macmillan, 1966.

Thatcher, Tom (ed.). *What We Have Heard from the Beginning: The Past, Present, and Future of Johannine Studies*. Waco, Tex.: Baylor University Press, 2007.

Vasari, Giorgio. *Lives of the Most Eminent Painters, Sculptors, and Architects*, trans. Robert N. Linscott. New York: Modern Library, 1959.

Via, Dan O., Jr. *The Ethics of Mark's Gospel in the Middle of Time*. Minneapolis, Minn.: Augsburg Fortress, 1985.

Via, Dan O., Jr. *Kerygma and Comedy in the New Testament*. Minneapolis, Minn.: Augsburg Fortress, 1975.

Via, Dan O., Jr. *The Time It Is: A Play About Jesus*. Lanham, Md.: University Press of America, 1982.

Vidal, Gore. *Julian: A Novel*. New York: Vintage Books, 1964.

Wasserstein, Abraham, and David J. Wasserstein. *The Legend of the Septuagint: From Classical Antiquity to Today*. New York: Cambridge University Press, 2006.

Weeden, Theodore J., Sr. *Mark: Traditions in Conflict*. Minneapolis, Minn.: Augsburg Fortress, 1971.

West, Cornel. *The American Evasion of Philosophy: A Genealogy of Pragmatism*. Madison: University of Wisconsin Press, 1989.

West, Cornel. *Democracy Matters: Winning the Fight Against Imperialism*. New York: Penguin Books, 2004.

West, Cornel (ed.). *The Cornel West Reader*. New York: Basic Books, 1999.

Wilder, Amos N. *Jesus' Parables and the War of Myths: Essays on Imagination in the Scriptures*. Minneapolis, Minn.: Augsburg Fortress, 1982.

Wiles, Maurice. *The Spiritual Gospel: The Interpretation of the Fourth Gospel in the Early Church*. New York: Cambridge University Press, 1960.

Wilken, Robert L. *John Chrysostom and the Jews: Rhetoric and Reality in the Late 4th Century*. Berkeley: University of California Press, 1983.

Williams, Steven, and Gerald Friell. *Theodosius: The Empire at Bay*. New Haven, Conn.: Yale University Press, 1994.

Wrede, William. *The Messianic Secret*, trans. J.C.G. Grieg. Cambridge, England: Clarke, 1971.

Wright, Wilmer C. (ed.). *Julian* (3 vols.). Cambridge, Mass.: Harvard University Press, 1996.

Yoder, John Howard. *The Original Revolution: Essays on Christian Pacifism*. Scottsdale, Pa.: Herald Press, 1977.

Yoder, John Howard. *The Politics of Jesus*. Grand Rapids, Mich.: Eerdmans, 1972.

Yoder, John Howard. *The Priestly Kingdom: Social Ethics as Gospel*. Notre Dame, Ind.: Notre Dame University Press, 1984.

Young, Frances M. *From Nicaea to Chalcedon*. Minneapolis, Minn.: Augsburg Fortress, 1983.

Zaleski, Philip, and Carol Zaleski. *Prayer: A History*. Boston: Houghton Mifflin, 2006.

Louis A. Ruprecht Jr. is the first holder of the William M. Suttles Chair in Religious Studies at Georgia State University. The author of five previous books, and over fifty scholarly articles and popular essays on a variety of religious themes, his work focuses mainly on ancient Greek history and culture, as well as the appropriation of those literary and philosophical traditions by later people, from the Romans to the Romantics. He has taught at a number of the most prominent religion programs in the United States and has been invited to give lectures and interviews in countries around the world. He lives in Atlanta, Georgia.

INDEX